I0840218

Search Engine Optimization (SEO)

By

E. Veazie Gilmore

TU ENTERPRISE PUBLISHING
FOUNDED 2019

amazon.com/author/bgilmore

Cyber Laws

The relevance and strength of our existing laws need to be always reviewed to experience the danger steaming from cyber reality. In this chapter, we are going to first identify the computer forensic, cybercrimes, and the cyber forces of the engineering challenges. The purpose of this chapter is to function as the catalyst to increase consciousness involving machine forensic which remains to develop as one of this most significant division of discipline.

Cyber-crime is a phrase that encompasses a broad variety of computer-related illegal actions. Examples of such illegal actions include identity theft, cyber intimidation, and business crime among others (Harmonizing cyber police and Regulations). Over these years' cybercrime has become the danger to increased technological progress. Hackers and IT experts utilize these loopholes in these data systems to employ their victims. In the finance level, the vice may imply exploiting customer databases and pilfering intellectual property. These are prime targets for hacking actions because of this business wealth at banks. force otherwise known as " cyberspace police " in the field of philosophy that governs how people use the internet. There are cyber forces that are illegal laws and there are cyber forces that represent national laws. Any force or control that effects how people have computers, smartphones, the internet, and other similar technology is cyber police. Cyber force is any force that uses the net and internet-related technologies. Cyber police are one of the newest fields of this judicial system. This is because internet technology evolves at such a fast rate. Cyber police offer legal protections to people using the net. This includes both jobs and ordinary citizens. Knowing cyber philosophy is of the utmost importance to anyone who utilizes the net. Cyber police have likewise been referred to as this `` force of the net. "

Cyber forces affect all Americans daily. Corporations large and smaller, as people rely on cyber lawyers. This discussion about cyber laws remains on the local, state, and national scale. Cyberlaw gives attorneys the chance to be a part of this language and practice in an interesting and different legal specialty.

Freedom of speech is an important field of cyber philosophy. Even though cyber forces prohibit specific behaviors online, freedom of speech laws also allows people to communicate their brains. Cyber attorneys must inform their customers on the limitations of free speech including laws that require obscenity. Cyber attorneys may also protect their customers when there is a discussion about whether their activities consist of permissible free words.

The important field of cyber philosophy is freedom of speech. Even though cyber laws require specific behaviors online, freedom of speech laws also permits people to communicate their brains. Cyber attorneys must inform their customers on the limitations of free speech including laws that require obscenity. Additionally, cyber attorneys may protect their customers when there's a discussion about whether their actions represent permissible free speech.

Cyber police relate to any laws about protecting the net and other on-line communication technologies. To call this rapid growth in cyber-related crimes, the government realizes that cyber forces need to be, revamped if needed to meet these challenges. The Ministry of Science, engineering, and design have gone with Cyber Security since last year to investigate cyber forces and all related forces and suggest amendments if required.

To preserve harmony and co-existence in Cyber Space, the necessity was thought for the legal government which we call `` Cyber police ". In simple words, cyber police are the force governing and controlling the cyber area. Cyber forces influence every aspect of the Cyberworld to be it Education, Entertainment, eCommerce, etc. and are regarded as fundamental forces of Cyber Space.

Cyber police are the part of the general judicial system that deals with the Internet, and their various legal matters. Cyber police cover a pretty wide field, encompassing various subtopics including freedom of speech, access to and use of the Internet, and online privacy. Generically, cyber force is referred to as this force of the net.

Put differently, Cyber police may be regarded as a part of the general judicial system that deals with the Internet, eCommerce, digital contracts, electronic information, and their respective legal issues. Cyber police cover a wide environment, encompassing various subtopics including information protection, digital transactions, and electronic communication.

These Cyber forces law covers predominantly the processed information (counting information protection and electronic exchange) viewpoints and it has been depicted as `material laws for the culture ". Cyber police or Internet law is a term that represents the legal issues described with the usage of the Internet. It is less a specific area of philosophy than the licensed design or contract law, as it is an environment encompassing many ranges of law and control. Some way themes include web access and usage, protection, the possibility of voice, and purview.

The computer-generated reality of cyberspace is called the internet and these laws prevailing its country. Cyber forces and all that users of the area come under the ambit of these laws as it carries a worldwide jurisdiction. Cyber police may also be identified as the branch of philosophy that deals with legal issues associated with the usage of inter-networked information technology. In brief, cyber police are the force regulating computers and the internet.

Consumers rely on cyber forces to protect them from online crime. Forces are created to prevent identity theft, credit card theft and other business offenses that occur online. Someone who commits identity theft may encounter ***Confederate*** or state criminal complaints. They might also experience the civil activity taken by the person. Cyber attorneys get to both protect and act against allegations of crime using the internet.

The Internet is rising nowadays but some people have become victims of hacking, stealing, cyberstalking, baby soliciting, etc. Which represent different types of cybercrimes. Cybercrime is committed at the net. Lawmakers, enforcement, and people need to learn how to defend themselves and those people for which they are accountable. The following represent several types of Cybercrimes.

Like any law, the cyber force is made to help protect people and organizations on the net from malicious people on the net and help keep rule. If someone breaks the cyber law or regulation, it allows another person or organization to act against the person or get them sentenced to the penalty. There are other kinds of penalty dependent on the kind of cyber force you broke, who you hurt, where you broke the law, and where you go. In some places, breaking the rules on the site can result in the account turning into suspended or censored and the IP address stopped.

Cyber ethics and cyber forces are also being developed to prevent cyber offenses. Every person must understand cyber ethics and cyber forces so that the increasing cybercrimes shall decrease. Protection delicate wares like antiviruses and anti-operative wares should be installed on all computers, orderly to be safe from cyber offenses. Internet Service Providers should also offer a superior level of safety in their hosts to make their customers safe from all types of viruses and malicious programs.

Reactions to malicious cyber action would include enforcement or diplomatic, economic, or military methods as appropriate for these conditions. That might include, but is not limited to, offensive cyber capabilities that break, refuse, or demean the computers or computer networks of opponents. Foreign diplomat Julie Bishop

edited by experts at computer safety, cyber investigations, and counterterrorism, and with donations from expert investigators, legal experts, and enforcement masters, Cybercrime and Cyber Terrorism investigator's reference can serve as the greatest respect to the modern times of Cybercrime. Cyber Crime and Cyber Terrorism investigator's reference is the critical tool in this arsenal of day's computer programmers, students, and researchers. As computer networks grow ubiquitous throughout the world, cybercrime, cyber terrorism, and cyber warfare must turn into some of the most interesting issues in nowadays.

The rising threat of cybercrime is true and important. This current breed of illegal actions and offenders at the cyber areas also present enforcement officials and prosecutors with topics and challenges at the investigation of cybercrime and prosecuting cybercriminals. While there is a large and growing structure of writing on cybercrime, there exist also research gaps that want to be addressed. In the section, we describe and suggest five salient and relevant areas of investigation that we think represents an enough foundation to further our knowledge and education on cybercrime, (Akers,1998).

Change with these trends of crime throughout history has been a slow start. Unfortunately for Enforcements, they are usually on the rear end of this and are frequently behind for months before being able to weaken these crimes. Cyber offenses are nothing new. Cyber Crimes are the recent and constantly evolving kind of crime that bases its whole plan from taking advantage of its victims over the internet. Enforcement's responsibility is to evaluate and get to prevent these crimes but it's not that simple. These cybercrimes are hard to combat in most instances

According to Petrocelli (2005), cyberstalking crimes represent the specific situation to enforcement, especially to those departments that lack the expertise or resources to analyze and pursue cyberstalks. Local enforcement is at a primary disadvantage because of jurisdictional restrictions (Petrocelli 2005). Here is an example of a claim that some victims made who went to the police for assistance, but were poorly advised to, just turn the machine off and that the mistreatment would end. The FBI has, in exchange offered to help local and government enforcement at tracking and pursuing cyberstalks (Petrocelli 2005). lawyers may be as guilty attorneys, or they may work for the office that produces and enforces national laws. National prosecutors may have complaints of national cyber law violations. Government attorneys general and local prosecutors also have complaints of violations of cyber police. In addition to criminal lawyers, government lawyers may be for authorities that implement cyber laws and encourage the public to use the internet in good ways. Lawyers at the U.S. Assembly and their staff may also play a significant part in arguing and making national cyber laws.

Bullying will pass this road into harassment, including cyber threats and cyberstalking. Threatening to harm someone is a cyber menace. Criminal forces against creating cyber threats exist in place. Cyberstalking is repeated harassment, using the Internet to go and maintain someone in a threatening manner, which causes the person to look very afraid.

Personal lawyers also work for customers in all areas of cyber law. They protect customers facing government and federal criminal charges. If the customer experiences a disagreement involving the cyber contract or domain purpose, they may rely on their cyber attorney to discuss that conflict or navigate related proceedings. Because of these jurisdictional challenges involved in cyber police, lawyers who assist their customers with cyber litigation may need to be careful when making their argument. They need to learn the principles of the Civil process, as well as look at the principles of information to effectively make their argument with admissible information.

At first blush, the force seems a fair attempt in tackling two areas of policy in need of movement. This beginning is cyber-security. Corporations in industries deemed to be important must immediately ensure that their application organizations are "safe and controllable." They must keep valuable information locally and would be subject to audits by official inspectors. Some law firms believe that firms should remain acquainted with many principles when using business reasoning regulations on cyber-security and how they are more important than those found in the new law. (the Economist., Jun. 2017)

The other neglected area brought on by the force is information privacy. Firms in other places have long accumulated and manipulated consumer information as they get access to it. As Ronald Cheng of O' Melveny, stated that the American police firms, remarks, that on-line crimes, malware, and mobile-phone scams are prevalent. Under these current regulations, corporations must be much more cautious with information that is developed by other people. They are required to keep a lot of information on local servers and must get permission before publicizing false information. (the Economist., Jun. 2017)

The much-anticipated Cyber safety forces (CSF) can expect to grow by 1 June 2020. These current laws are the first broad law to address cyber safety concerns at the federal level and to some extent consolidates cyber actions caught in different laws and rules. The decision by the U.S to beef up its laws and rules regulating cyber action is not different from what is occurring around the world. However, deciphering exactly who is caught and what is hidden is giving companies uncertain as to how they can comply with the vague and possibly burdensome law. (control Risks., May. 2017)

Global legal matters of cyber-attacks are complicated in the world. Even if the antivirus business locates the cybercriminal behind the existence of a specific virus or part of malware or kind of cyber fire, much that local governments will not act due to a lack of laws under which to prosecute. (Ted.) (hack at this Box protection Conference.) Writing attribution for cybercrimes and cyber-attacks is one great issue for all enforcement agencies.

We see this Chief Counsel as having a vital part in reducing the organization's cybersecurity risk. These laws and regulations in cyber safety are constantly changing, with best practices frequently turning into regulations. Two New examples include GDPR in EU and New York state's part of financial assistance regulation 500, which need organizations to establish compliance with cyber government requirements by demonstrating robust, structured and documented cybersecurity programs. (Skroupa, C. P., Feb. 2018)

The Global cyber coalition (GCA), the business of enforcement and research organizations focused on combating general cyber danger of seriousness, important ways established by the New York County District Attorney, The City of London cop and the center for net safety. (Wintermeyer, L., May. 2017)

The commission stated it has dominion over this fed's cybersecurity because this committee is tasked with the management of the U.S. National Association of Standards and Engineering, the authority responsible for developing federal cybersecurity standards and guidelines, Under the 2014 government information technology law. (Reuters., Jun. 2016)

In the U.S we have several rules about cybersecurity and information privacy. The Cyber administration will make real progress in enhancing our corporate cyber resilience without necessarily pushing for further laws or rules. (Beshar, P. J., Nov. 2016)

This lack of quality at this definition of CII is important because of the possible responsibilities for these corporations, for instance, localizing information to the public and undergoing intrusive onsite inspections of cybersecurity systems and procedures. Specific technologies must give the "public safety assessment" to ensure they will not be illegally operated or interfered with before CII operators can use them. The CSF gives comprehensive agency to the internet government of U.S, strong internet watchdogs, and other business regulators to conduct these reviews, (Control Risks).

SEO As We Know It

(SEO) is this abbreviation for web search engine optimization. 'Search engine optimization (SEO) is the process of involving the profile of a site or the page in the web search engine's physical or organic search results. ' The highest-ranked site that is exhibited in this search results database receives the number of visitors from the web search engine's users. (SEO) help to make sure that the website is available by the web search engine. 'Search engines are programs that seek documents for specific keywords and take the list of documents where those keywords were discovered. ' Research engines change users to seek documents on the website.

What is a web search engine Optimization person online and digital marketer consultant by night? Google finds to be the most common web search engine for getting products, data, and services. To grade amongst the best outcomes of Google and different search engines, e.g., Bing and Yahoo, (SEO) tend to be the most used resource. (SEO) personnel will help you achieve your goals of being visible to those looking for your business or services. Be cautious of quick fixes as it may be detrimental to the online profile and impacts the business negatively. Web search engine optimization must be done right. SEO expert Brad ensures that with his companies the site can rank among the great web search engine outcomes!

The broad explanation is that web search engine optimization is the art and science of creating web pages appealing to search engines. More narrowly, (SEO) attempts to pull specific elements known to change web search engine position to create specific pages more appealing to search engines than other web pages that are competing for the same keywords or keyword phrases. The purpose of (SEO) is to make the page superior web search engine ranking. The greater the page's web search engine optimization, the higher the ranking it can reach in search result lists. (say that (SEO) is not the only element that defines web search engine page ranks.)

This is particularly important because most people who have search engines just see the first page or two of the search outcomes, so for the page to take up communication from a search engine, It gets to be named on those first two pages, and the higher that position, the closer the page is to the first list,. And whatever the page's position is, you need the site to be named before your competitor's websites if the business is selling products or services on the internet, Nevertheless, demystify web search engine optimization or (SEO) first advances your visibility. Simply put, it is the procedure by which the site or webpage earns more views. I’m pretty sure you need more people to see your work; This is a nice way to do that. Furthermore, the more search engines give the page exposure, the more visitors can see. Moreover, through optimizing your website, you gain more organic traffic regularly on your website. This means that you will get more traffic from Google and other search engines as well.

There are also other search engine specific category types like (***Spanish* SEO**). Nevertheless, remember that Spanish web search engine optimization, called Spanish (SEO), is the process aimed at improving the quantity and level of communication to the Spanish websites from search engines via "natural" search results. Search engines go to be the center focal point when it comes to marketing the organization on the internet because a large amount of these specific visitors to the network site can find you mostly after conducting a keyword search. Using a search engine of their choice like (Google, or Bing) can increase your sites traffic as stated earlier. You can sometimes use keywords like, pictures, and books to modify your site in theses search engines, e.g., Google, Yahoo, Bing and thus improve your search engine rankings. (SEO) is the method adopted to rank the site well in web search engine results. It improves the quantity and level of communication to the site from different search engines.

You should modify the website to fulfill the users' needs. One of those users is the web search engine, which helps other users find the knowledge. Web search engine optimization is about helping search engines see and present knowledge. The website may be smaller or larger than our example website and provide a vastly different message, but the optimization issues we talk about should refer to websites of all sizes and types. We hope this book gives you some fresh ideas on how to market your website, and we'd like to see the inquiries, feedback, and success stories at amazon.com/author/bgilmore.

Search Marketing is the procedure of improving the profile of the site at search engines. It includes Web search engine optimization (SEO) and web search engine commerce (SEM). (SEM) is the process of optimizing the site to make more essential communication from search engines. While web search engine Marketing is entirely about purchasing targeted communication via pay-per-click search ads. It's a way to increase traffic by increasing the number of visitors who visit.

As its name implies, Search Engine Marketing is the knowledge of marketing sites and web pages for a breakthrough at search marketing and, more obvious location on search engine results pages. This is achieved through the kind of ways, from what is called “on-page” (SEO) to “off-page” techniques. On-page (SEO) refers to best practices that network content makers and website owners will take to ensure their knowledge is as easily discoverable as possible. The web search engine marketing expert oversees improving web search marketing rankings for sites. They will choose suitable keywords to aim in their web search making optimization campaigns, the sites using a variety of (SEO) tactics.

This site improvement activity mainly consists of publishing keyword-centric content, as well as marketing page titles, line tags, alt tags, and meta tags. They also guarantee that the general design of the site enhances the user experience. (SEM) Specialists so examine the strength of the (SEM) effort and change their strategy accordingly. Off-page improvements is the part of (SEM) techniques. (SEM) (web search engines marketing optimization) is split into 2 components, on-page, and off-page marketing. On-page improvement comprises of name tags, Meta statement, Meta tags, HTML tags, the composition of URLs, and the concentration of keywords. For successful SEM efforts, one must employ the best digital selling companies in web traffic agencies.

eCommerce (SEM) — web search engine marketing (search engine marketing is the activity while the user classifies one word or speech into the seek engine, a sophisticated set of principles returns the list of net pages.

They are all ranked in the order that the highest relevant results be at the pinnacle of the page. The most site visitors — higher than 60 percent — get to the main three physical positions on the first SERP. This is where search engine optimization comes in.

Almost 80 percent of people say that “name recognition” is the #1 reason they go on the search result in the web search engine like Google. You might be doing everything just to modify the website for search engines marketing through (SEM). But if they don’t realize the brand thanks to powerful branding, they’re not possible to move the site.

The purpose of web search engine optimization is to get the search engine spiders not just see the website and pages but also specifically rank the author relevance so that it looks in the top of the search engine results. This process of improvement is not a one-time process but involves fixing calibration, and constant testing and observation.

If you're not acquainted with it already, its immediately experience is to see SEM. Web search engine Marketing involves using keywords to take in organic web search engine results and change the web search engine ranking. Suppose you have a pizza parlor in New York, NY. You need to be able to look within the opening two pages of Google search results when hungry New York-based clients do the hunt for local pizza parlors.

You've probably seen web search engine marketing or (SEO) earlier. You've probably seen somewhere that it is better for business and that it can make the site well seen in search engines like Google. (SEM) systematically process the website more web search engine friendly and related to the number of keywords that relate to the industry. It's the constant process that if done properly will generate great amounts of benefits for the business. Why do we want to apply this knowledge for our business? The infographic this is what makes natural free web search engine marketing and search engine optimization management easily through magazine article content. The web search engine optimization organization causes great rankings extremely rapidly. There is one trick though to achieving higher natural search engine optimization rankings, this is accomplished by referring the special keywords to any of these magazine article entry websites while the piece is unique. If not, you will be impacted by their duplicate content payment.

Knowledge has other side benefits. Google hates secrecy. Thus, making digital knowledge on the website, journal and other online assets are crucial to optimizing for search engines. If you want to be in search engines when people write in those important words and phrases, take the art and study of web search engine optimization.

Since there are billions of sites on the internet and people have search engines to get them, the fundamental knowledge of web search engine marketing (SEM) is crucial. Writing allows you to modify SEM. This includes using the exact keywords in the book, having plenty of connections, making useful writing pages and URLs, and using pictures and videos.

Site owners recognized the value of the higher ranking and clarity in web search engine outcomes, (searchenginewatch.com.) Making the possibility for both white hat and dark hat (SEO) practitioners. According to business expert Danny Sullivan, the saying `` web search engine optimization" probably came into usage in 1997. Sullivan credits Dr. Clay as one of the first people to propagate this period. (Sullivan, June 14, 2004) On May 2, 2007, Jason Gambert tried to mark the term (SEO) by convincing the marketing business at Arizona; that (SEO) is the `` knowledge " involving the use of keywords and not the `` selling service. "

Search engine crawlers may see several other elements when crawling the website. Not every author is indexed by these search engines. The length of pages from the root list of the website may also be the factor in whether pages go crawled. (CHO, J., Garcia-Molina, H., 1998)
Some search engines have likewise handed out to the (SEO) business, and represent common supporters and guests in SEO conferences, webchats, and seminars. Leading search engines provide data and guidelines to assist with site improvement. (google.com.) (bing.com.) Google has the Sitemaps system to help webmasters see if Google is having any problems indexing their site and offers information on Google traffic to this site. Bing Webmaster tools offers the choice for webmasters to apply the sitemap and network feeds, this allows users to define the crawl rate and follow the web pages index status. Search engines may punish websites they find using dark hat methods, either by shortening their rankings or

eliminating their lists from their databases entirely. Such punishments may be used either automatically by the search engines' algorithms, or by the manual website assessment. One instance was the Feb 2006 Google separation of both BMW Germany and Ricoh Germany for the usage of misleading exercises, (Cutts, Feb 4, 2006). Both corporations, however, promptly apologized, limited the offending pages, and were restored to Google's database. (Cutts, Feb 7, 2006)

In March 2006, Kinder Start filed the case against Google at web search engine rankings. Kinder start's site was removed from Google's list before this case and the quantity of traffic to the website dropped by 70 percent. On March 16, 2007, this United States District authorities for that Northern region of California (San Jose) ignored kinder start's objection without permission to revise, and partly granted Google's motion for Rule 11 sanctions against kinder start's attorney, requiring him to give a portion of Google's statutory expenses.

(blog.ericgoldman.org.)

On Oct 17, 2002, search King filed a case at the United States territory Court, Western region of Oklahoma, against this web search engine Google. Search King's assertion was that Google's tactics to keep spamdexing represented the tortious obstruction with contractual relations. On May 27, 2003, the court allowed Google's motion to ignore this objection because search King failed to submit the right upon which assistance may be given." (Docstoc.com. May 27, 2003.) (Olsen, May 30, 2003)

Companies that use too aggressive techniques will make their customer websites banned from the search results. In 2005, the Wall Street Journal reported on the corporation, communication force, which allegedly used high-risk techniques and failed to expose those hazards to its customers. (Kesmodel, Sept 22, 2005) Wired press reported that the one organization sued blogger and (SEO) Aaron

Wall for writing about this prohibition. (Penenberg, Sept 8, 2005) Google's Matt Cutts subsequently confirmed that Google did prohibit commerce force and some of its customers. (Cutts, Feb 2, 2006). Bing was brought into this list of search engines available at Opera application from v10.6, but Google continued the options web search engine.

Microsoft scores search agreement with theater Software Mozilla Firefox created the agreement with Microsoft to collectively publish Firefox with Bing's, the version of Firefox where Bing has replaced Google as the default web search engine. (Bing.) (Mozilla). This basic version of Firefox gets Google as its default web search engine but has included Bing at its database of search providers since Firefox edition 4.0. (Sullivan).

Nowadays, most people are looking at Google using a mobile device. (Google.com.) In November 2016, Google announced a great change to the means crawling sites and began to get their list mobile-first, which means that the moving version of the site grows the starting point for what Google includes in their index. (Definition.net.)

Some business owners move their on-line organization's SEO campaigns that same way. They think that website improvement initiatives are applied only if the website launches and that the benefits reaped from these first tactics can remain evergreen and never need updates. (Gray, M., Jun. 2018)

Search engines are created to help users get the data they want. They are optimized for hunt and typically provide specific methods such as full-text search, complicated search manifestations, and ranking of search outcomes. (Brown, M. S., Mar. 2018)

What should savvy online organization owners be doing to ensure that they stay competitive and at enterprise? For starters, stop the attitude that (SEO) is a one and done to-do list work. Web search engine optimization should be the cornerstone of the comprehensive digital marketing program that includes regular customer practice and participation. This effort must be trackable, measurable, analyzed, corrected and fully responsible for all results. Customers should have to be made aware of planned and new site optimization jobs, initiatives that have been implemented and how productive each is and has existed. (Gray, M., Jun. 2018).

The History of SEO

Web search engine history all began in 1990 with Archie, the FTP website hosting the index of downloadable list listings. Search engines continued to take primitive directory lists until search engines evolved to crawling and indexing sites yet making algorithms to optimize relevance. Google's specific and improving formula has given it one of these most common search engines ever. Different search engines continue to have a tough time fitting the relevancy algorithm Google has made by studying several factors, social media, inbound links, and fresh knowledge. Customer history, of the great web search engine optimization service provider gives their best to meet customer's purpose. The consumer history talks a lot about the business and what sort of tasks they can control. When you investigate these items it will tell you the brief about their potential and whether they will help you to survive in a competitive market or not.

The difficult issue with writing the history of web search engine optimization (SEO) is the vague etiology of its first. By choice, the term web search engine optimization means that the difficult aspect of the inference is the fact that search engines and the Internet did not always take their modern structure. For instance, the Internet arguably will trace its origins back to 1958 when AT& T introduced the first commercial modem, enabling distant computers to transmit around common phone lines.

Search engines continued to take primitive directory lists until search engines evolved to crawling and indexing sites yet making algorithms to optimize relevance. Google's specific and improving formula has given it one of these most common search engines ever.

Search engines have become the ubiquitous component of this online education for millions of users. The web search engine book accurately evaluates the important importance of web search engine optimization to eCommerce success with the statistic: 93 percent of the online process starts with the search. Avoiding web search engine optimization would quickly put you in the number of online experiences, a condition which would be fatal to the eCommerce goals. The (SEO) strategy: Web search engine optimization is the efficient process of pleasing the search engine crawlers or bots. Various strategies, tactics, and techniques deployed to draw the search engines to list and rank those network pages easily. The prime purpose of doing SEO for the site is to increase the traffic to the site through greater exposure in web search engine results page (SERP). White hat and dark hat represent the two fundamental varieties of (SEO) techniques

Additionally, Microsoft gave Verizon telecom USD 550 million (see, Dianne, Jan 7, 2009) To take Bing as the default search supplier on Verizon's BlackBerry and let Verizon go off (via BlackBerry delivery books) these different search providers are accessible. Users would even find different search engines via the mobile application. (Searchengineland.com.)

Most network search engines are commercial ventures supported by ad income and so some of them provide advertisers to get their lists ranked higher in search results for the fee. Search engines that do not receive money for their search results get money by doing searches like advertisements alongside the usual web search engine results. The search engines get money every minute somebody clicks on one of these advertisements.

What (SEO) is though, is the critical element of the general digital marketing strategy, and one that needs to be made right for maximum strength. The person in charge of the web search engine optimization effort will make or break the whole digital campaign. (Olenski, S., Jun. 2018)

In October 2011, Microsoft said that it was running on current back-end search infrastructure to present faster and somewhat more pertinent search outcomes for users. This current index-serving technology had been integrated into Bing globally since August this year. (web search engine watcher. 30 Sep 2011.) In May 2012, Microsoft announced another redesign of its web search engine that includes `` Sidebar s", the cultural characteristic that searches users' cultural networks for data related to this search query. (Goldman, king, May 10, 2012)

Web search engine optimization is the art and science of writing data in the format which can make search engines think that the knowledge satisfies the needs of their users for related search queries. (SEO), like search, is the area often older than I am. It was not originally named web search engine optimization, and to this day most people still do not know where the phrase came from.

Making Money Using SEO

From how to create a website online and knowing how to get money selecting the right place. Involves finding the right keywords to making use of the best (SEO) techniques. Wealthy organizations had everything the entrepreneur wanted, and these are just the ideas from a single class! You will need to maintain in touch with these businesses and make the greatest indications on how to overcome the pitfalls that may occur will allow you to understand the concepts of making money using these business opportunities.

Search Engine Optimization is one of the most important online accomplishment you can learn to help your business grow. You can receive a lot of money from your business if you master the (SEO) methods because it allows you to move your posts to the first page of Google, break up lots of available tasty traffic or get the bank on the organization of drop shipping. We first began selling Cryptocurrency in

January 2016. We went out with $ 9000 that I scraped collectively on credit cards and was able to take that into almost $ 350,000 at under the year. This was a significant turning point for TU Enterprise. People who already use (SEO) services, most likely already own a website; Moreover, they understand how they were getting wealth from it. Significantly, this also meant that they had the money to spend on (SEO) companies and got some baseline measures to determine the individual advance. They would think driving traffic from searches could make them a return on their assets, and then they were looking to change this. And this only meant greater quality and the more on-time paying customers.

Being a businessperson, we already realize the value of being visible in Google search engines. But for some owners, before they spend money on (SEO) optimization, this important question remains the same: How (SEO) will improve my business? We have jotted some easy tips that'll help you grow apparent at Google hunt.

Brighton (SEO) formulated a large conference and there were a lot of wealth sloshing about in the SEO business. We have existed to huge technological conferences like OSCON, but tickets for conferences like this are costly. Brighton SEO was available for most attendees, but they needed lots of generous supporters. To me It was a waste of money for proposals, we have seen 99 percent of (SEO) corporations out there and they are only preying to get the fast buck off uneducated beginners. DO NOT spend money with the (SEO) organization UNLESS you search this business yourself and get a reasonable degree of understanding of what the companies you are purchasing entail and how they will benefit your rankings.

The entrepreneur or freelancer has two important schemes to use when marketing online. Web search engine Optimization (SEO), which tries to rank the site on search engines “organically”, and web search engine commerce (SEM), which places the site in search results in exchange for money. Both strategies will be used to make the job successfully—but which one is good for you?

We heard about one-page SEO (web search engine optimization), off-page SEO (web search engine optimization) to make clarity at Google page rankings for having more engagements, but these 5 points which we are talking about in this book or handbook per say made SEO tips greater for customers. Furthermore, to maintain healthy relationships with these existing customers and to get new recurring customers, by changing the TU Enterprise using word of mouth.

There are a bunch of definitions of SEO (written web search engine optimization in the U.K., Australia, and New Zealand, Or web search engine optimization in the United States and Canada) but essential SEO in 2018 is even largely about having available communication from Google, the most common web search engine in the world; The website needs to be obvious and visible is what we think of when we think about Google. Around 90 percent of online experiences start with the web search engine, so the site needs to be optimized for the best web search engine optimization practices. When you select our site design company, you're ensured to have a site optimized for (SEO).

One of the most significant and manual methods of optimizing the productive eCommerce site is making certain it's optimized for search engines. With present's web search engine optimization (SEO) measures, it's now more critical than ever to confirm the site is always updated with rich and relevant content, promotes a good user experience (UX), And is optimized to remain as error-free as feasible.

The recent metaheuristic optimization formula, called cuckoo hunt (CS), was produced recently by Yang and Deb (2009). The article presents a more comprehensive comparison study using some basic test functions and new designed stochastic test purposes. We then use the (CS) formula to solve engineering design optimization issues, including the designing of springs and welded light structures. The best results received by CS are far greater than the best results received by the effective particle swarm optimizer. We can talk about the specific search characteristics used in CS and the implications for more research. (yang, X. S., & Deb, S., 2010)

In 1998, two postgraduate students At Stanford University, Larry Page and Sergey Brin, produced Backrub s, the web search engine that relied on the numerical formula to measure the prominence of web pages. The figure estimated by this formula, PageRank, is the use of the amount and power of inbound connections. (Brin, Sergey&

author, Larry, 1998) PageRank calculates the probability that a given page can be hit by the network user who randomly surfs the network and is links from one page to another. As result, this implies that some connections are stronger than others, as the higher PageRank author is more likely to be hit by this random network surfer.

Net search engines themselves predate the beginning of the network in Dec 1990. This Who is an individual hunt date back to 1982 (ietf.org.) And this Knowbot data Service multi-network user hunt was first applied in 1989. (cnri.reston.va.us.) This initial great documented web search engine that searched knowledge files, namely FTP files was Archie, which debuted on 10 Sep 1990. (Deutsch, dick, Sept 11, 1990)

Technological improvement makes the page appealing to the web search engine and ensures that the website has no broken connections with any error codes (like 404s). Otherwise, this reference would be badly ranked by the web search engine. Optimizing URLs and creating this slug -- everything after the .com -- concise drives the web search engine to discover the related subpages and categorize the other components of the website. That is critical to the success of any (SEO) effort. These technological (SEO) elements help the UX and are present to advertise the message. (Sharma, K., Jul. 2018)

The price you pay on (SEO) is engineering opportunity price: “what were the engineering’s feeling if they wouldn’t’ ’t focus on (SEO)?”. If you go ads you might make a great Return on Investment, but once you stop spending money, the communication stops coming in. Once communication is set up, it is more than likely to always work on communication. It places for semantically relevant keywords, “what to do at whatever the index page is per attractions or what to do per action. This is Google’s Hummingbird formula: “ranks matters, not strings: this means pages will rank for subjects today, not only one keyword.

All network site owners would like to be in the number one position in the greater search engines. To accomplish this, some attempt to modify their websites so they can attain higher page ranking. The search engines set principles for web search engine optimization (SEO) ; for instance, webmasters are not supposed to add hidden text, make contact exchanges with irrelevant websites, etc. (for example, to carry one's list keywords with words like sex, drugs, and rock 'n roll, even though this website might take about the new science textbook.) Some contend that these practices-called black-hat (SEO)-undermine the justice of these outcomes.

Given search publicity has not existed without conflict and the topic of how search engines present ad on their search result pages has been the aim of the series of surveys and reports, consumerwebwatch.org June 30, 2003 by user study Web Watch. The Federal exchange Commission (FTC) also released the letter (ftc.gov. June 22, 2002.) In 2002 about the value of disclosure of paid advertising on search engines, in response to the charge from advertising Alert, the user support group with ties to Ralph Nader.

Companies That Benefit From SEO

Long Term success optimizing your site can make you continued wealth for years to come. Cultural media advertisement and PPC advertisements last if you are feeding wealth into those structures, but (SEO) for nonprofits builds upon itself endlessly improving daily. Equally you can make more keywords, content, and updates continuously will help your business establish the power of the web and the number of visits you receive regularly. You end up remembering where you came from before you will remember where you're going; This is defiantly true for (SEO). Before you optimize your website for the best presentation, you will need to do a complete site audit to determine the actual website's knowledge, function, code, and keyword density to determine site strengths and weaknesses. So, we set up the tools needed to follow the measures that can produce performance outcomes of the website and help us optimize over time.

The common topic in the web search engine optimization business, defining the timeline for (SEO) outcomes will be a difficult process. After all, no two sites exist just alike. It will be challenging to recognize when (SEO) changes can change into benefits, particularly because of hindrances, sites that have been penalized, technological issues with troubleshooting, compliance authorization, or even wait-times for cooperation from Its departments. It's also important to see how different marketing communications will impact (SEO), including paid search and reputation management, and ensuring the site design is produced with best practices. Whatever this barrier, (SEO) needs team effort and a practical timeline that provides for both long-term marketing strategy and short-term website jobs. Web search engine analysts work meticulously to get new issues, keep future website issues, and improve the website quality. Mostly, all sites start to find the change within the first six months of improvement. Below is a more detailed analysis of the practical (SEO) timeline:

Create a well-designed website with interesting patterns, too as related pictures so that it shows up rapidly with these searches. Also, focus on the composition and knowledge of the system along with the (SEO) and keyword because they're important for website clarity. (SEO) is likewise cost-effective and offers long-term important benefits. It also maximizes the clarity and size of the organic visitors to this site.

(SEO) is critical for the effective run of the website. Web sites with more than one writer will help from (SEO) directly and indirectly. Their primary benefit is the increase in web search engine traffic and their second performance is having a general structure (checklists) to have before writing content on the website. Because of the ever-increasing popularity of the internet and social media, some companies are putting a substantial part of their budget on web search engine optimization. Some companies have been seen investing in (SEO) because if they do not, their competitors will overcome them.

Today (SEO) may not be useful without well-executed content curation, this is where cultural media kicks and it helps you unlock untapped possibility. Compared to different selling communications, social media benefits (SEO) in surprising ways. It's not surprising that (SEO) and SMM have turned easily into close intertwined actions that all businesses need to benefit from. But how just will SEO and (SMM) business together? Do social media signal change people's websites profile at Google? We have been investigating this matter for some time now and here's what we have learned thus far:

Paid search advertising is huge business ($ 52 billion for Google only in 2015), then consider it to stay around for a time. Businesses struggling with ranking up organically with (SEO) or current sites help from using paid search ad to increase exposure to the related audience to become seen on the first page of the search results.

To take effective outcomes from this site, it's important to have a specific (SEO) strategy running for you. Realizing the necessity benefits of (SEO), developers do not take back in investing the considerable quantity to make desired results. Nevertheless, it's important to see how these (SEO) service providers help to develop the site in search results before seeking their assistance. There are some free alternatives out there but it's nice to know what is best for you and the site.

You may get regarded as our journal post a couple of weeks ago about (SEO). But to summarize, (SEO) stands for "web search engine optimization" and relates to the site's unpaid (or "organic") rank in web search engine results. 75 percent of users never move past the initial page of search results Thus, (SEO) is a big deal. Do you want to take the organization on the first page? So, you'll want to provide the strength of social media. Google offers real-time social sharing in search results, so the organization's social media reports are indexed within the best of some results. Sites are known to be left unaffected for months, or stillages.

Another point of generalists represents (SEO) copywriters. At the minimum, (SEO) copywriters learn how to incorporate target keywords and phrases into web text to increase organic search performance and prevent penalties. Some may still use keyword research (if scoped in this work). Naturally, (SEO) copywriters are just the authors you need when you desire to produce knowledge to improve the website rank better organically in search results to bring more traffic to your website.

Dejon (SEO) also identifies itself by providing (SEO) education services. They intend to teach whole marketing and promotion departments about the benefits of (SEO) and to create the combined strategies. This is particularly useful for larger corporations, who would frequently already have the network that designed a vision but might not have a clear (SEO) strategy or understanding of how (SEO) will help their business.

(SEO) and that social media selling are completely inseparable. Web search engine optimization is the marketing field that suggests developing visibility in organic web search engine results. Using that (SEO), brands will modify themselves to increase their visibility and quality largely linked with social media marketing. If you don't know the client, you will not be anything to them! Social media allows both to know the client and the client to remember you. Put differently, jobs and clients may understand each other easier thanks to social media. Still, to be a successful in (SEO), you want to see how social media and (SEO) work together. While having the message shared on social media may not provide immediate (SEO) benefits, the secondary benefits are immense. As the message becomes shared by more people, you get increased communication and gain more chances for having links; and these do get a primary (SEO) performance. (Rampton, J., Sep. 2016)

We recognize that connections from social media don't always go through (SEO) benefits. Nevertheless, there are some reasons why social media should take part in the (SEO) strategy, including increased visibility, communication and engagement/connection with the people. And Finally, these will have a substantial effect on the search rankings. (Rampton, J., Sep. 2016)

Some (SEO) traditionalists have taken a time to realize the real benefits of social media as it pertains to the essential search marketing strategies, but social media does far more than just ensuring the organization is keeping up with this competitor. Social media gives corporations an extra platform to interact with customers, develop their brand, and make up a community, all while also taking traffic to their site. For more on these benefits of social media and precisely what it is, think “what constitutes social media selling, and How will it improve your website?” (DeMers, J., Jan. 2014)

Optimizing and engaging within cultural networks has not always been the purpose of SEO but should remain. While SEO efforts are primarily performed to attract new clients and increase awareness of the job within essential search outcomes, social media focuses on keeping clients and strengthening relationships with them through strategic engagements. (DeMers, J., Jan. 2014)

These were good to emphasize that both SEO and social media take important characters in digital marketing strategies. SEO, cultural, content growth, PPC [Pay Per Click, they all want to be together, " said panelist Craig Lister, chief of commerce agency Reprise Media. (Anderson, T., Jan. 2014).

How To Use SEO

This conversation goes off only with questions on how to use (SEO) handles, and how to use (SEO) to promote a brand. This is where the bulk of articles regarding (SEO) on how to use a hashtag, though some were not immediately in reply to using in their first post. While I loved the beginning of the Twitter conversation that we had, we did not feel as though we had more to accomplish until midway through this communication.

Today, we have the legitimacy strategy of the (SEO) business because in the online reality there exist two broad types of (SEO) Black-hat (SEO) and white-hat (SEO). White hat (SEO) increases search rankings from real hard work and information. Black hat (SEO) requires questionable methods that may take you to the top, but not for long and these tactics are usually detrimental to the long-term growth right.

Okay, but not actually, frankly, it is super difficult to tighten up (SEO) rankings. You will probably be in high positions unless you have black-hat (SEO) exercises. Black-hat SEO exercises comprise of frowned-upon tactics to trick search engines to grade the site. Yet, you should not care about that for any reason, because you are going to hire a trusted (SEO) organization working for you. Once you reach a high position, you should switch to using different keywords.

Firstly, there's white headdress (SEO). White hat (SEO) relates to those tactics and techniques that constitute search-engine sanctions. These strategies outlined here at the guide are all white hat (SEO) schemes; they understand these guidelines search engines get placed in place to assist their users and give them with high-quality content. Squeezing the content full of keywords is not a good way to increase the SERP rating. One, spammed keywords tend to seem artificial or forced which increases the jump rate of the author. Two, Google is quite great at getting (and penalizing) spammy websites.

(SEO) has shifted and It doesn't recognize knowledge for this purpose of keywords anymore. (SEO) in today's reality goes down to structure and level knowledge more than it does keywords. And that is a good thing for audiences. It implies that instead of publishing mountains of knowledge, our current ends should be about making more value out of less knowledge.

We see that many (SEO) experts tell that (SEO) is the "technological thing is key because without the technological support (SEO) is a lot harder, and for certain types of websites this is impossible. As (SEO) masters, we frequently clock and split knowledge from reach and technological (SEO), but neither constitutes about (SEO). They both exist, and it's okay for them to be one or the other. But for goodness sake, you do not have to take both to use (SEO). However, this knowledge is based upon that if you do not write, you cannot be good enough for (SEO) according the many people we have interviewed.

(SEO) is a structure, layered subject. There are various types of (SEO) and some factors that may affect (SEO). An experienced (SEO) advisor can help you determine the kind of SEO that is crucial for the business. That can be influenced by the business you're at, the geography at which you control, and the (SEO) strengths, weakness, opportunities, and threats of the analysis.

This knowledge of (SEO) has changed the fortunes in various jobs, and their success has laid the groundwork for the development of the (SEO) business. (SEO) is not the short-term result for business income. Rather, (SEO) is the long-term marketing strategy and should be incorporated into different facets of advertising the job; Over the last few years, we've had this chance to work with clients from a plethora of industries. We've yielded stunning outcomes for their jobs and we did this by keeping the clear reporting system.

Local (SEO) is a mess to focus on. It's constantly changing and will take a lot of time and effort to go well. That is why then many (SEO) agencies and consultants specialize at local (SEO) rather than wider (SEO). These principles are very different as you're aiming to accomplish other goals, and in some cases, customers do not care if the higher profile of their jobs in local search and job listings directories leads to more immediate communication and foot traffic than website visits.

When you select a (SEO) authority, search for one that is focused on the goals of your business. Some corporations offer matters, e.g., on-site (SEO) and mobile optimization, but not site redesign or local (SEO). Some (SEO) Companies in Fairfax will give almost everything you want. For example, if you are running a building or a plumbing job, you should concentrate on a specific geographic client base. Therefore, you want companies that concentrate on local (SEO). You may see this content on their websites. Yet, you are free to touch them through the telephone.

Platinum (SEO) is the Melbourne (SEO) company that focuses on moral and important (SEO) companies. Their squad facilitates increase communication, conversions, and sales. Platinum (SEO) provides powerful low-cost (SEO) software programs to its clients. Platinum (SEO) provides specific and professional site care software to manage their customer's site and keep it updated. Their network care companies are tailored to meet their customer's needs, whether you want the site Hosting and Website help they are willing to update your site so you can focus on growing your online business.

When the business approaches professional (SEO) companies, they can be offered with custom (SEO) services. This implies that they can be offered with the importance of results that have been individualized to satisfy their online requirements for success. They might require email marketing companies, site development, and innovation services, web search engine optimization services, campaign management services or any other services that can increase their online presence.

In this competitive world of commerce, it is like the struggle to show the spirit of a company online. Having the greatest position for the website, (SEO) is essential for corporations. (SEO) is the abbreviation for web search engine optimization. The process aids in showing the name of the organization in the search result when searched at Google, Bing or Yahoo. To avail the ultimate benefit of on-line commerce, GATT is the greatest (SEO) delivery provider in India.

Upon entering this world of on-line advertisement, we were bombarded by three text acronyms (TLA). Every measure and procedure appeared to be taken at least one for us to see, what we would get out of (SEO). Every web search engine uses the algorithm to decide what websites show up and what requests they are presented from what was seen. (SEO) is the practice of business and promoting the site to be put as the best result. I listed a couple of below as I think they are helpful in both implementing and knowing (SEO). The individual intention is playing a higher part in how search engines rank web pages. For instance, if the person is looking for (SEO) companies, is the person searching for articles on how to make the (SEO) organization, or are they searching for a listing of (SEO) companies that provide the service? In the example, the latter is more probable. Even though there is a little possibility that the person may be expecting to get the (SEO) job, Google (with their impressive information on individual habits) realizes that the vast majority will be expecting to see a listing of companies. All of that is made into Google's formula.

Conferring with the (SEO) person is important because these experts are the agency in using (SEO) marketing tools. They get an understanding of the processes of (SEO) and learn how to use (SEO) tactics to help businesses achieve enhanced site communication and business development. While the principles of (SEO) are not rocket science, this useful aspect of (SEO) for businesspeople can be the quality that they will not deal with because of these technological elements concerned with its application. That is why (SEO) corporations are pursued after.

Today (SEO) is the powerful way of making business more productive. At closing years (SEO) turned into one of the most common ways of business effectivization. (SEO) requires making or changing the Web website in a sense that makes it 'easier for search engines to both crawls and list its message" (Beel, Gipp, Wilde, 2010; Google, 2008). It takes time, knowledge of (SEO), and successful execution of these desired on- and off-page (SEO) elements to modify the site for higher rankings at search engines. If the corporate strength of the website or the individual page's (SEO) is more effective than all others, with regards to the question, you'll rank # 1. Because (SEO) requires so many ranking elements, you may remember the #1 website as winning a triathlon of sorts. In the true triathlon, the success of the moving part is not necessarily the winner of the whole contest – and therefore it is the same with (SEO). When you take these running site designs in this book, (SEO) companies and (SEO) Experts can help develop a broad (SEO) scheme or help support the existing (SEO) enterprises to make the site to rank on top of all Search engines including Google, Bing, and Yahoo; as the content (SEO) advisors do this On-Page improvement, You can be held informed of all the (SEO) developments as these (SEO) Experts understand the rightful ways of web search engine optimizations that are not attempting to deceive the search engines.

What does (SEO) put for in secular's statements? In brief, (SEO) stands for 'search motor improvement'. This is the procedure of improving the site's ranking on Google hunt and different search engines. (SEO) helps people see the site in the middle of the billions of different websites that exist. This concept that Quora shows up first is the prime example of (SEO) in force.

(SEO) WP is the (SEO) focus idea created in 2014 that was newly updated. It was made for (SEO) authorities that works to take the case of their (SEO) campaigns. It includes superior (SEO) plugins to assist better (SEO) and page-loading. It includes segments for case studies, marketing available books and resources, the platform page model, forms, and more. It was described as the greatest (SEO) WordPress idea for 2015 on Theme Forest. It’s a good option for (SEO) and marketing agencies.

Both Yoast (SEO) and All at One (SEO) gets a bunch of choices. This makes the way seem a little daunting. Both plugins make their greatest to change matters and create it easier for users to set up their (SEO) backgrounds. We think that Yoast (SEO) does a somewhat greater work than All at One (SEO) with their multi-page and tabbed backgrounds.

Not only does (SEO) overlap with individual experience in a larger manner, but it also greatly overlaps with content marketing. Some (SEO)s fail to find any substantial change between (SEO) and message marketing. In this case, a day of (SEO) is subject selling. (Patel, N., Apr. 2016). These are not the needs of changing what SEO can constitute, but they can alter how (SEO) will be accomplished. (DeMers, J., Mar. 2018)

In these times, webmasters are finding it difficult to work out what can be critical for (SEO) and what's no longer applicable. To explain further the significant trends in the (SEO) business, we published this book (Search Engine Optimization, (SEO) to dominate the year 2020, In publications on (SEO) Education to easily understand this subject matter.

Is SEO Needed?

If 2019 was the year you realized that you would need a website that is ranked, then 2020 would certainly be the year you would need (SEO) services. As it's become easier and easier to make sites, the only choice for the site to stand out from the others is understanding web search engine optimization. One of the greatest classes I've seen to get from 0 to 60 at (SEO) is the Click Minded (SEO) class that is popular and taught by the (SEO) coach from PayPal and Airbnb.

When you select the (SEO) authority, search for one which is focused on whatever you want. Some corporations offer matters, e.g., on-site (SEO) and mobile optimization, but not site redesign or local (SEO). Some (SEO) Companies in San Jose will give almost everything you want. For example, if you are running a building or a plumbing job, you should concentrate on a specific geographic client base. Therefore, you want companies that concentrate on local (SEO). You may see this content on their websites. Yet, you are free to contact them through the telephone. We learn this in a way that is (SEO). We learn these tricks of the business needed to increase websites to the top level of (SEO). And to go with those at the top level of (SEO), there are procedures to incorporate into the (SEO) model. Integrating powerful off-page (SEO) techniques into the site to increase the search result ranking is a method of them.

To best understand why you want to add (SEO) into the digital marketing strategy is because you want to remember what (SEO) is. (SEO) or web search engine optimization is the usage of keywords and different elements on the site to rank for searches on the search engines. This is free when done by yourself and will change the amount of essential communication when you go to the site.

But like every other business who have core values, likewise, they have different (SEO) motivations. Holding that at the center of our work, we plan a specific (SEO) strategy for every customer we work with. We also think that an intelligently applied (SEO) strategy will create a strong web presence for the organization by targeting the right people.

This way would cover the two important components of great (SEO) On-site knowledge of technical (SEO). Any pro (SEO) could immediately reap the benefits of integrating a great (SEO) service and is most likely to do well from it. More (SEO) work is required, but under the resource constraints mentioned above can kick-start the Organic process in the right way.

For the whole (SEO) strategy to work, you want to surround yourself with good people. Nevertheless, you must realize that the (SEO) strategy is a long-term strategy. According to Forbes, it takes at least four months for the great (SEO) marketing strategy to begin making outcomes. The comprehensive (SEO) strategy should be applied by experts, search engines make more than 200 components to make their ranking; it can hardly be managed without content.

If you are very interested in improving (SEO), the strategy needs to be developed. The individual would want to determine the companies or products that take the most revenue for the business so he can deploy an (SEO) strategy using the current business model. Keyword investigation is needed, as is onsite (SEO) optimization. If you have too many keywords shoved into the domain, that may be regarded as a spammy tactic that Google will get on. Including the keyword within the organization is a great exercise though, if it is a physical way, certainly. Let's say I wanted to make the trade roofing company.

Nowadays, as we shift from Poacher to Gamekeeper, we are concentrated on serving many corporations like yours by getting the best (SEO) corporations to fit the specific needs of other companies. Each of them can provide a variety of (SEO) assistance from (SEO) Audits to keyword research to link building services and more; below we share with you our insights and insider knowledge as to what you need to know, What to search for and how you should evaluate (SEO) suppliers for each (SEO) assistance.

Out of all this SEO toolbars available in this industry, (SEO) is likely the most effective, and deals with the magnitude of design choices — so you will configure it to adjust to your (SEO) needs. Apart from providing the boatload of information for every URL you see, you will also do basic on-page audits, analyze domains, and trade the information.

Searching for a reliable web search engine optimization company to accomplish the work can have many turns. We curated the list of these major (SEO) corporations to help you get the right provider for the (SEO) needs. Each organization is ranked using the Clutch method including, detailed customer interviews, ratings, and in-depth business investigations. Consider the best companies to see which (SEO) provider is best for your work.

To accomplish hunt finding ability and (SEO) prosperity, you'll want expertise and activity from oddballs, marketers, networkers, salespeople and more. (SEO) makes time, but it's that long-term assets. Advertisements are faster, by trying to have the business getting paid today, but (SEO) pays off huge in the long term, like the retirement program. All-important corporations should do (SEO), hunt advertisements and social media. When we explain (SEO) to people who are not common to the (SEO) business, we normally have them, follow these instructions; we encourage businesses to get modifications to their websites and commerce to help ensure that when people search for them on web search engines like Google, they are searching for issues involving with their products and services.

When we frequently use the (SEO) acronym; we sometimes forget that it stands for web search engine optimization.

(SEO), in its heart, is the procedure of making sites more convenient and comprehensible to search engines. It shouldn't take, and truly doesn't want to be looked at as manipulative, (DeMers, J., Nov. 2013).

A lot of people believe that web search engine optimizations (SEO) is a business service, like e-mails, desks, and staples. But SEO is not something every business wants, particularly small businesses with moderate selling budgets, (Shorr, B., Jul. 2018).

Why Do We Use SEO?

Conferring with the (SEO) person is important because these experts are the agency in using (SEO) marketing tools. They get an understanding of the processes of (SEO) and learn how to use (SEO) tactics to help businesses achieve enhanced site communication and business development. While the principles of (SEO) are not rocket science, the useful view of (SEO) for businesspeople will be the quality that they will deal with because of these technological elements, as it relates to these applications. That is why (SEO) corporations are pursued after.

Much overlooked from one's (SEO) training is the basic understanding of search engines and their business model. Some (SEO) professionals concentrate on the short-term activity and result (SEO) tactics. They ask: "If we make the difference to the site, what will happen?" The significances of setting the long-term (SEO) strategy requires one to answer these questions:

Today, the complexities of the once-understandable environment appear overwhelming at best. Having to absorb this knowledge of algorithm adjustments while attempting to be on Google's great position is equated to gaining an advanced degree in sciences by some. How are you supposed to use good (SEO) strategies to get your business off the surface when you don't see the (SEO) environment from the beginning? (Adams., May. 2016) Entrepreneurs cannot even reject (SEO). It's critical to the well-being and prosperity of the business, (Patel, N., Apr. 2016).

As Google extends to unhinge selling models everywhere, corporations are increasing expenditure on digital marketing companies. If you are considering investing in web search engine optimization (SEO), it may be difficult to determine where to spend money, particularly when selling budgets are usually hard. However, (SEO) firms may have a lot of value to the business, and some marketers are taking the plunge. According to media analysts in Borrell, (SEO) expenditure can get $ 80 billion yearly by 2020. (Harrison, K., May. 2017)

One great challenge the entrepreneurs face is their need for knowledge about how (SEO) has shifted and what the means for them and their job. (Patel, N., Apr. 2016)

Personal (SEO) results: (SEO) is not like purchasing a piece of material that you can make if it does not suit you. SEO is an important asset that will either increase the business or destroy it. We recognize the importance of appropriate (SEO) for the job. In CENITPRO, we firmly believe that every sector has its specific necessity and challenges and we offer customized and best-suited (SEO) solutions for the job.

What Will Be The Future Of SEO?

(SEO) as we would expect! tells us that (SEO) is just a "technological thing. It's an excellent idea because without the technological support (SEO) is a lot harder, and for certain types of websites this would be impossible. As (SEO) masters, we frequently clock split knowledge from reach and technological (SEO), but neither constitutes what (SEO) really is. They both exist, and it's okay for them to be one or the other. But for goodness sake, you do not need both to get results.

Marketing professionals believe that (SEO) is the lifelong of a flourishing powerful marketing campaign.

(SEO) is growing increasingly competitive, and mostly because of the large quantities of knowledge being created daily. Google's algorithms are also growing more intelligent, and, we believe that the future of (SEO) can mean privileging knowledge that's well-written. Page scraping can search for elements, e.g., sentence structure, and be more rigorous with the level of the images and pictures contained in posts as well.

“The future of (SEO) can encapsulate the uniquely holistic approach to interpreting online search behavior. With this power today captures data points as granular as anyone may think, success in (SEO) would require a comprehensive understanding of information analysis, individual behavior, and elements of what’s now known as technical (SEO). As (SEO) comes to grow and voice search grows more of a value, we can find less of the dependence on keyword-focused strategies and let the paradigm shift towards the user-first approach in marketing.

“I believe that the time of (SEO) rests in a similar area as the history of (SEO). While there are constantly ‘dark hat’ and problematic techniques that may be used to dupe these search engines and make temporary higher rankings; due to long term (SEO) prosperity birthed to great content. Moreover, the messages that people need to see addresses the searches immediately and deeply, this is astonishingly good that people will demand it. Google needs to add value to the lives of those people that take it by answering their search questions correctly and practically. This book covers this issue so deeply that no one would ever need another book on this subject by taking the best.

The time is unpredictable, but in this world of search, change is the number. For that reason, search marketing can continue to remain a priority for those who want to be competitive on the network. Some people claim that (SEO) is gone, or that (SEO) totals to email. As we find it, there's no need for a team except simple systems like websites vie for aid. These positioning in the search engines, and those with this knowledge and experience to change their site's ranking to have the benefits of increased communication for clarity.

Teaching about this history of (SEO) is urgent. That is because of the concept that it would provide new (SEO) experts to think about how search engines can alter when the net is emerged. Nevertheless, helping them forecast the future of the internet in a pretty accurate way. After all, knowing where something came from can inform you where it is going to start because you make the understanding of its flight. The info below, made by TU Enterprise, will inform you all about the history of (SEO). Sure, things will never change at (SEO) and the purpose of users, search engines and (SEO)s. Search engines move, and individual habits change, and therefore (SEO) can move along with it. Business professionals sometimes relate to these changes as if the demise of (SEO) were present; this is not at all the case. Like all things, it's just developing. (Gleeson, B., Apr. 2015)

One of the best ways to achieve that is through (SEO) (web search engine optimization), organically getting the website to the place of search results for relevant keywords. This (SEO) operation requires a bunch of moving components,

some of which are experts. Furthermore, some companies that are geared toward performing well on Google typically employ a (SEO) master or an agency, (Pinsky, 2017).
Even laying the foundation for better performance in search can give dividends long into the future. Going out with an (SEO) friendly website innovation will prevent duplication of efforts in the long term and make it faster for the next (SEO) organization to get your company in better rankings, (Willi, 2017).

Is Your Work Outsourced?

When you outsource the job, you do not have to care about the preparation recruitment expenses. You only want to look out for the companies' quality of their past tasks and half of the job is done. Within outsourcing, you get access to more skilled work at a very low price. It is usually seen that people opt for outsourcing as a great source to get access to the quality accomplishments of the business. As it helps to determine the greatest human resources from the people.

You should simply outsource the business that comes out of the organization's expertise. For instance, if you get the bakery, then outsourcing any kind of IT needs would sound reasonable. If you're an IT company, outsourcing the IT business would seem bad. Outsourcing should be made to keep you and the employees from missing focus on the fields of expertise.

Nearly every aspect of the modern-day job will be outsourced. Take all the ways you believe in outsourced resources for the job already. Do you outsource legal and business jobs? What about enrolling? We are convinced you've outsourced business needs to FedEx or UPS on time, right? Tens of thousands of jobs rely on outsourcing to help back-end sector purposes and processes; and However, it's even difficult for some business leaders to take the benefits of outsourcing sales and marketing. Outsourcing isn't always about sending businesses abroad. Business will be outsourced to different jobs within your group and outsourcing will be a huge resource to small businesses attempting to develop. Here are some benefits the job will find from outsourcing and three tips for making it productive. Only one person acting poorly at work will direct company morale into a downward spiral. Alas, most corporations take more than one-do-well taking everyone else down. It's the moment to tell that morale- and productivity-busting personalities on the rug so you will mark them and steer light of their lot.

Some outsourcing companies still work within the same times as the business does to ensure that the job is done in a timely way. Frequently, people working in an outsourced organization will produce the goods within record time, giving you a better opportunity to concentrate on the things that matter to the job. Change is usually a great thing and for corporations who spend a bit much time doing a specific job that isn't at all important. Outsourcing is a good choice to make the business process easier to manage. Those working at a local organization may decide to outsource a portion of their business so that they will continue to concentrate on the core business operations.

In this field of call center outsourcing, organizations that are not known at working with outsourced call centers may suffer from lesser end-user-experience as the result of outsourcing. This is exacerbated when outsourcing is mixed with offshoring in areas where the initial word and society are distinct. (Nadeem, S, 2009)

Corporations have been outsourcing business for some years. At outsourcing, specialized companies offer their services to consumer companies at lower costs than the computer companies would do the business in-house. Outsourcing the business to international or sea companies, only to benefit from lower labor rates in those countries, turned into called offshoring.

You may take outsourcing to one or more freelancers; affect them as well as any good human could affect their employees. These are those people who are developing the strategy that works for you. If you attempt to invest in the team then it will appear in the outcomes. (Patel, N., Jun. 2016)

Outsourcing includes both international and domestic contracting, and sometimes includes offshoring (relocating a business function to a remote region) or nearshoring (transporting the business operation to a closed country). Outsourcing is often confused with offshoring, yet, they can be described: The company may outsource (work with the service provider) and not offshore to a remote region. For instance, in 2003 Procter and Gamble outsourced their installations ' organization assistance, but it did not require offshoring. (center for English development. 2012-07-09.) Both involve remote work that some CEO's and high managers appear to fear. Most of these out staffed companies are offshore, and here's the reason it's important to hire an offshore company to increase the personnel. Offshore outsourcing or out staffing means getting the good talent from different nations, but not the owner, as staff determines it. Most of these American firms frequently outsource IT companies to be competitive.

It's a general idea that outsourcing and offshoring are the same matters. The main differentiator between outsourcing and offshoring is that offshoring constitutes one form of outsourcing. Offshoring is when the business employs a third-party firm to do business in a country different than one where the enterprise mainly conducts its operations. The business model evolved from outsourcing, as corporations looked for cheaper alternatives to companies abroad, normally in the developing countries of India, Bangladesh, or Eastern Europe.

Unlike conventional outsourcing strategies, companies are now producing business models that allow outsourcing in some areas of the business's strategy, including activities like research, innovation, and development. The new rise of 'offshoring ' and outsourcing talks of a more refined way beyond standard actions driven by cost-saving.

Outsourcing is the newest buzzword these times, as increasingly value and quality conscious jobs all around the globe are working to destinations like India for outsourcing their non-core job processes. So, what exactly constitutes outsourcing and what are the benefits of getting the offshore person to do the job for you? The most evident and obvious performance refers to the cost savings that outsourcing explains. You will get the work done at a lower price and on a greater level. Because of the change in salaries between western nations and Asia, the same sort of work that is made, it will be made in India at a fraction of the cost.

Look at your process and look at the efficiencies to recover experience through outsourcing. Take yourself and the staff Blasingame's Outsourcing Power Question: Must the work be made in-house? The response can be from this question, (Blasingame, 2016).

As you assess the outsourcing options, keep in mind that there are rewards to outsourcing and disadvantages of outsourcing. See each one of the outsourcing disadvantages listed below and determine what effect could take on the business and its process. If these outsourcing disadvantages outweigh the rewards of outsourcing, you should prevent outsourcing those processes. Rest in mind that some purposes or departments give themselves often easier to being outsourced. Therefore, what would be a liability in one sector may be an advantage for another

Yet, while there are some benefits of outsourcing, there are some drawbacks and specific circumstances dependent on where and how the business is outsourced. The organization may get into communication issues in domain content. In other words, if the preferred outsourcer is less familiar with the business, you should provide additional time for some training. Conventional outsourcing business-like business and philosophy have overcome the situation by setting up exercises that specialize in vertical industries. The most obvious instance is that of the outsourced team working at various time regions with a substantial language barrier. spite of saving money, corporations have frequently experienced unexpected drawbacks from outsourcing, e.g., miscommunication or lesser level of intermediate products, which end up delaying the total creation process. Another reason for the change in outsourcing is that some businesses that were subcontracted overseas have been replaced by technological advancements. (the Economist n.d.: N. Pag. 17 Jan 2013.)

One disadvantage of outsourcing the software development team is that they might be working on different tasks directly together with the work. Nevertheless, higher-level software technology outsourcing companies offer dedicated, full-time resources for the work, so the team works closely with you, and just you, one-on-one, within your business hours. That gives you greater power over the job the outsourced team does and ensures you take the point and results you need.

Keep in mind that outsourcing the recruiting is distinct from outsourcing the cause resources, as the second may add benefits, compensation, worker and labor relations, and legitimate matters as well as the recruiting. Although outsourcing the recruiting to the recruitment activity outsourcing business includes a cursory feel and the revision of those facets, outsourced recruiting typically looks in the hiring procedure from sourcing good candidates to the new employee onboarding process. Price system and the need to concentrate on core business processes are at the top of the list of some general causes to outsource recruiting. Outsourcing all the recruiting or simply a portion of the recruitment process places the reins at the hands of skilled recruitment advisors, saving you time and money. Different reasons employers prefer to outsource recruiting include the need to change recruiting procedures, reduce the higher turnover rate, control fast development or seasonality that makes it impossible to stay up with hiring needs, develop competitive advantage, And organize recruiting and on-boarding. We bet you would like to know how does Outsourcing, and Offshoring have to do with (SEO)? Well it does, because that is exactly what you are doing when you are using (SEO) services. Most of the time you are designating a portion of your business services to be source by another company to help develop your business strategy.

How Long Does It Take To See Search Results?

It takes time to develop a strong foundation for the long-term affiliate business. It takes time to increase the confidence of the people and the search engines. It takes time to find early results. It takes time to develop the organization income into a full-time income. It takes time to measure the business to a higher degree that exceeds the whole-time revenue umpteen times.

How long would it go to look if it was worth it? Often something is worth doing if you will make the sense of success (or not) come quick. But sometimes it would take months to find the effects. If we don't remember for the period, is it even worth it? Anything we would do to reduce the moment of knowing? What variables aren't at our power? This figure usually comes up when talking about partnerships or integrating with the outside world. What components can't we keep? What are these opportunities something changes materially that might radically change the trajectory of this program? Is the risk worth getting? How do we think about this right?

The careful or long answer to the question would take time to respond, as there are hundreds of factors that influence search results. Google's search algorithm is very difficult, changes often, and is not entirely understood to the world. In the next chapters, I can dig deeper into some of the important factors that influence search improvements, but for now, we will only go with my simple summary of the key components of (SEO) success.

What if you do not get in-house HTML architects? You can find complex matters while converting Photoshop designs to HTML. The result is outsourcing that transformation. Outsourcing the job to specialists would be a time saver. If you do not have significant exchange requirements, there are no cause glowing holes in the pocket. You will save the funds by outsourcing these periodic conversions.

Safety will not be outsourced. As the industry, we want to prevent confusing outsourcing signing keys with outsourcing protection. But working over signing keys and process commands to the third party cannot protect you or your clients from stealing. We need opt-in safety measures, like CCSS, and yearly safety audits. First and foremost, we want to concentrate on understanding these dangers and accurately explaining them to users.

Analyzing the web search engine results: Make's suppose that we do the search at Google to "save money." You will find that most search results are (SEO) friendly (and targeted keywords), But some of these headlines themselves are not appealing to these people. Adding a long tail to this name might help for those with proper questions. The Google Panda 4.1 news was designed to punish "skinny" or superficial content, by preventing bad content from ranking highly at Google.

Google recently updated its web search engine effects to appear higher at search of these effects that are somehow part of the Google world (feeling YouTube, Google+, blogger). What Google writing does is to refer the Google+ profile with the journal (therefore you can find your pictures at these search results) and this can make it a higher priority result in a search query with your name. You've almost surely heard of DuckDuckGo. It's the preferred option for Google's web search engine. Thinking in the supremacy of Google to get out related search results, I resisted using DuckDuckGo for some time. Yes, sometimes it's important to get the viewer that remembers the past searches, knows where you are at spacetime and tells you how some effects there are for the given search (3,700,000 results in 0.59 seconds!). But generally, you only need the topic answered or that one webpage to pop up at the top few results.

Google yourself. Use our available software to examine new search results for your family. Make note of all positive, harmful and irrelevant search outcomes. Yet if most effects are positive and crucial, you should also take note of search outcomes that you will control, and those issued by different companies. Modify the brand. Even though you're currently at a good position with your online presence, that does' 't ensure that the attributes are optimized. Perhaps you have a specific family, and there's never been anything bad or unwanted published about you. If that is the case, it's easy to turn into inactive, Do not! Sometimes all it takes to ensure the online existence is to write the name into Google. If you find outcomes that determine your brand, act on it immediately. Take the web search engine to remove these pages from its effects by following the simple process. Notice that Google has distinct operations designed for important outcomes and Google Images.

Although it’s been a portion of the Google search page since the earliest times, some people do not even learn what the I’m Feeling hot button does. It’s very easy – it only brings you to the initial search result found for the keyword. Pushing the button with the keyword entered automatically opens the opening page at the search results. Then it will be a convenient route to use, and today there is one way to set up the Google Chrome search box (otherwise called the code room) to search with I’m Feeling Lucky.

When you do keyword hunt it researches both quantity names and quantity descriptions also seller's secret keywords, so you turn out with lengthy search outcomes. In contrast, if you hunt by name it searches for single goods family and it does not hunt quantity descriptions or marketer's obscure keywords, you will turn out with more targeted and short search results.

Large search engines that make the searches have the information to provide ads and to "personalize" the search results. When the search engine's formula considers the browsing history and previous advertising clicks, it filters the effects. That means that the outcomes you think are specifically tailored towards what you're most likely to go on. Even if the search results seem incredibly valuable and crucial, the search engine is not serving you fair, verifiable and objective search results. That is referred to as the "filter bubble". See More: What represent device Bubbles and How to prevent them.

Google and different search engines have machines learning to change this search outcome for you. Every time you perform the search, the algorithms in the backend make the watch in how you react to the results. If you move the best results and remain on the page for long, the web search engine assumes that this the results it displayed agreed with this question. Likewise, if you get the second or 3rd author of the search results but do not move any of these outcomes, the web search engine calculates that the outcomes served did not match requirements. The means, the algorithms running in the backend change the search results.

Because MySQL does not get the optimizer and the process search questions each moment may take a longer time accessing this information to predict the effects, completed searches are cached in the DB as well. So, whenever this one search is made again, defined by the SHA-1 hash of the search sequence, the effects in the store are just returned, if they are present. To provide for alterations in system pages, each search store is likewise timestamped. When the timestamp of the search question is more than 2 weeks old, this method forces the fresh process of the search.

This installation of web pages is referred to as this 'Index', and it is the information storage that is organized and utilized to support the search results you find on the search engine. Categorization is the process of preparing these masses of information and pages so they can be searched quickly for related results to the search question. This formula is a very complicated and lengthy equation that calculates the value for any given place about the search period. We do not know what this algorithm is because search engines tend to make that one closely guarded secret from rivals and from people looking to play the web search engine to get to the top spots.

For better search engines, there exist almost zero switching prices for consumers. It's as easy as navigating to another web search engine, which does not cover its users and write the one question into the search room. Since personal search engines don't cover the data, the results may be less targeted, since usage of the information is how great search engines populate the results, But it gets nothing more than changing the web search engine you have to stop giving the information over to the better search provider, since great search engines are hard embedded with these.

Hubei, like other search engines on this database, does not make identifying individual profiles or create specific identifiers, but unlike the different search engines on this database, it is a semantic search engine, So it uses machines learning to assess the abstracted environment of these keywords, allowing results that were nearer to the users first meaning. Notice that these (SEO) companies take the privacy very seriously but is also a cold part of tech.

Web search engine, computer software often gets answers to queries in the collection of data, which might be a collection catalog or a database but is most commonly the Web. The search engine creates the list of "pages" — computer files listed on the Web—that contain these statements in the question. Most search engines permit the person to connect statements with and, or, not to modify queries. They may also see specifically for pictures, videos, or news articles or families of network websites.

(Britannica.)

Google has been complying with various petitions to make down search entries as long as those search outcomes are not at the national benefit. But until today Google has set that process to country-specific spheres, such as google.fr. The French regulators stated that this organization must make search results down across all its sites, (Matthews, 2015).

Google emphasized that this term could become thin and limited. These organizations remove sensitive data from its search results in a couple of different cases, such as when the result links to a person's bank account number or signature. And in Europe, Google now must remove more personal negative data about citizens thanks to the court judgment that enshrined the “position to be buried” online. (Luckerson, V., Jun. 2015)

Does this fall imply that Google is seeing tweets as less important to add in the search results? This could be. Google is always fine-tuning its algorithms to decide how to prioritize what shows up. (Rampton, J., Dec. 2016)
“We are saddened to find the hate organizations still exist. The fact that hate websites happen in Search results does not imply that Google endorses these views,” told the representative in the document. According to the organization, the website’s ranking in search results is defined by computer algorithms using hundreds of components to compute the page’s relevance to the given query, (Roberts, 2016).
Some (SEO) firms can tell you that it takes 4 to 6 months to get realizing outcomes. This’s generally correct but bear in mind That is when you begin seeing results, and (SEO) effects develop over time. Whatever results you’re seeing in 6 months should be substantially not as much as what you will see in 12 months. At some point, you may think

the effects taper off, and so it may be a matter of keeping outcomes rather than developing them, (Steimle, 2015). Rankings matter. But they're not the measure you should be concentrating on. If, by taking "How long does (SEO) get to begin running?" You think "How long would it take before I go high rankings?" So, you're mistaking outputs for outcomes, as Seer Interactive founder Wil Reynolds is fond of saying. Having rankings is the signal (SEO) firms may easily be because they're emotionally rewarding, but they're pointless unless they produce leads or sales --the result you want. This's a reason you should just employ (SEO) firms or (SEO) professionals who focus on results, rather than outputs, (Steimle, 2015).

Will I Have To make Changes To My Website?

We're the next phase of this web site is what you often here (SEO) firms say what trying to get your business. But the truth of the matter is you may need to make changes to you site to maintain organic outputs. You could have had 10, 15, or even 20 developers working on your website, but technology have changed so much it is now possible to make organic changes to your site with a simple drag and drop format. This process scales seamlessly. We bring new features and capacities every single period in order to have the greatest of both worlds. (Lashinsky, A., Sep. 2010)

One of those most notoriously over-the-line is that social-networking website called Tagged, in which the New York Attorney General Andrew Cuomo stated he projects to sue tagged for incorrectly publicly misleading commerce, along with identity theft, this is a perfect example of what can happen when the wrong, personal, or bad information is published on a social media website, (Atal, 2009).

Recently we revamped our site, which was difficult because I'm a web developer by business, not the web designer. Last-minute we did for a college course called creating and developing business websites for sport in 2009. We thought we might attempt to use some of this, as some of these trends back then (Adobe Computer Science Software!) Are today fashionable again. But we saw ourselves missed on Web Archives for minutes, thinking how the internet used to exist.

According to our previous experience returning customers are increased by 70 percent but simply because they enjoy our job. They constantly meet us for their current website design work, and we make them happy with our work. All these occur through web design through websites. These sites not just promote our ability it also connects me with the latest web design trends and technologies.

We think that our experience with technology, specifically in the web design area, give us the best score for the point.

At our previous work, we oversaw keeping and updating our company website. This involved keeping employee's profiles updated and continuously sending data regarding future events. We loved what we were doing, which is what drew us to the point with the organization. we would like to use the writing and content skills that were learn there to be used now.

We had enough experience to move into the portfolio and create our site because we could not afford to hire somebody. We built our site on WordPress and fortunately had the coding course at college as an elective. We were blessed. We learned how to make our website beautiful. And whatever we did not learn how to do — we googled it. we were awakened at 3 AM every night researching, education, YouTubing tutorials. Taking notes, hearing these codes, and tweaking. We did not wakeup because we had a job to do, we woke up because we were not going to go back into the corporate world running for a boss we did not do well with, and the hostile work environment that came with it.

Several years later, we realized that there were all these sites on the internet, and we needed to create our own. Then I googled how to do this and went on to do the session on codecademy.com. I made a small, rather awkward looking site. It was exciting — I had published something that I'd created, and the entire world would find it!

Some of these conflicts but resulted from the fact that we got to modify our e-mail. We indexed which sites were connected to our account, began changing our e-mail (after getting the new e-mail provider, yahoo), found some companies we completely forgot about and found out some sites make it difficult to modify the individual e-mail. We met various customer service departments. (This is related to how some websites determine the size of the password — ridiculous from the personal security perspective).

We told everyone that we got our "personal" site, but it was ours. We thought that only because our art was there, and we spent that moment making it seem the way we needed it, we would say it belonged to us and this was our website. But it never cost us any personal money. It belonged to this listing maintenance like Wix.com where it was hosted. We spent a lot of time there and got some connections and acquaintances, but one time this place was suddenly down, with no way to our portfolio. All our links were started, and we had to build. This could not have occurred if we had our own website and report from the very start.

We have always had a personal website, the first site I made was our site. So, we have had a private site since 2010, and we have always taken one loop or the other, we make changes to our sites mode when we think of it. Also, what is not great is we do not have the timeline of all those past patterns, but we are sure to remember something. We think it is only the net and being the creator, at that point we do not believe there should be tags like [amazon.com/author/bgilmore] when we are all on the Internet, or online. You will see what people in the world is doing, they will find what you are feeling, by doing this, there is simply no value.

Finally, once we learned to create our websites — and we were in education at that moment learning Mass Communication — people began reaching out and asked if we could make websites for them, design iPhone apps, or simply do designs. This is when we began freelancing and getting on any design work. Whether it's atoms or pixels, these rules are the same, and the point of development taught me that Essentially, innovation is about communicating.

Since we were no longer bloggers, but an author who (sometimes) blogs, we wanted to move our site accordingly. We dragged our feet because we put a lot of work into our journals —not only writing these stories but choosing the name and tagline; designing the logo; constructing this site; and figuring out the technology.

What Makes One SEO Organization Different from Another?

Like every business has other core values, Likewise, they have different (SEO) motivations. Holding that at the center of our work, we plan a specific (SEO) strategy for every customer we work with. We also think that an intelligently applied (SEO) strategy will create a strong web presence for the organization by targeting the right people.

If the organization figures out the good (SEO) practices so it will take 100x organic growth within the year. But instead of getting too technical and innovative, it is extremely important to confirm that the fundamental components of (SEO) are in place first. Things like crawling health, place listing, mobile readiness and page performances need to take order for the site. Searchability constitutes this use of crawl ability, indexability, and readability.

Line for (SEO): Our useful (SEO) way explains how to map the (SEO), site investigation, keyword research, competition analysis, on-page and off-page strategy that can improvise organic traffic and resulting clients. Our teaching method of (SEO) education in our organization presents delegations of how to use web search engine optimization. This project new ways of how to win over new customers, make sure existing customers are adept to find what they are searching for, and to create cost-effective and sustainable online commerce.

The socially entrepreneurial organization (SEO) makes the purpose of making cultural influence on a new level by using modern methods to coordinate, manage and evaluate the business. If you're expecting to benefit from the impact in this new cultural change field; enterprising your idea on how to prosper using a (SEO) would be a great choice for success. In this chapter, we will give you some tips on how to get the most out of (SEO) that will help you thrive, and still change the world.

It'll help make the decision easier to remember that there is not the thought of a tone ideal for a (SEO) company, but the ideal of the (SEO) organization for your specific business. Each of these (SEO) companies on our list specializes in something different, has a different operation, and are placed in several countries. With all these variables, you'll be able to get the (SEO) organization that is the best qualified for the job.

(SEO) is a subset of data structure. Most SEOs are uninformed about content structure. They always confuse data structure and technological structure. On the website, content structure is organizing, labeling and connecting knowledge so that it is easy to take and easy to make.

Usually, take the example ALT attribute and take in this form to improve the images rank as search engines may not "find" pictures. As a matter of fact, in the U.S. It is regarded the act of discrimination against those with a disability, as reported at ADA 508 (that Americans with disabilities act).

Not only does (SEO) overlap with individual experience in a large manner, but it also largely overlaps with content marketing. Some (SEO)s fail to find any substantial change between (SEO) and message marketing. In their minds, a day's (SEO) is subject selling, (Patel, N., Apr. 2016).

In this day in age, competing with different organizations' (SEO) rankings will be a challenge, and nearly impossible without the help of (SEO) coding. Our business invests in several instruments that make our businesses a lot easier and reduces our keyword research and optimization experience. Some of our favorites represent Moz, HubSpot's keywords way and Yoast, and Prosper Strategies. Businesses often remember (SEO) as a common set of techniques, when, the (SEO) campaigns differ widely by industry. In 2018, Google doesn't only provide three advertisements and ten essential outcomes: They provide answer boxes, local results, carousel papers, and more. Optimizing for each kind of outcome seems different, so you need to make your efforts depending on how the prospective customers see according to, Tim Chaves, from Zip Books business Software.

When you employ a (SEO) firm, confirm that they do more besides just optimizing the robots.txt and writing tags. They should be capable to offer quantity in (SEO) schemes (keyword research/focus), knowledge marketing strategy, and off-page (SEO) methods and knowledge, (Patel, 2016).

If the job serves a small or midsize market or a restaurant, then standard (SEO) would not be because the keywords targeting the industry will lack enough amount to produce the best ROI. For example, consider the local (SEO) campaign, which is a specific form of (SEO) involving other techniques that is considered valuable for the measure (that is, the national scope) (SEO) campaign, (Shorr,2018). The (SEO) effort can be monitored and carefully tracked to record the progress made and to change these various (SEO) tactics with the target to increase the online lead production. Important measures that can be measured include rankings, contacts, organic visits and target completions like form submissions and calls generated from this site.

Some organizations are just involved in (SEO) so that they will rank their knowledge rapidly and get some money in the short-term. Dark hat (SEO) requires tactics that focus on optimizing knowledge just for those search engines. This means that organizations are not considering the cause of visitors that can see and navigate their website knowledge. These organizations can turn or break These rules to change their website rankings to get to a quick buck.

There are a bunch of definitions of (SEO) (written web search engine optimization in the U.K., Australia, and New Zealand, Or web search engine optimization in the United States and Canada); but essential (SEO) in 2018 is even largely about having free communication from Google. This being the most used web search engine in the world and being the most single strategy used in the UK in 2018). (SEO) is another commonly used method of advertising affiliate product but also the most challenging. (SEO) is the process of improving the profile of the site or the page at search engines via this "raw" or un-paid organic or algorithmic search results. (SEO) does not get results directly, but it can be highly profitable in the long term.

Can SEO Services Increase My Sales Or leads?

Branes is the ideal place to take paid (SEO) companies in the United States. Our targeted and powerful (SEO) efforts help increase site communication, promote customer interactions and eventually help increase sales. We promise outcomes beyond expectations. As a major publishing company in the U.S., our skilled (SEO) team is decided to make the brand recognized on search engines. We carefully evaluate the requirements of our customers and give the best outcomes as we choose the quality at quantity.

Get the benefits of our greatest (SEO) companies at Google that makes you skyrocket your improvement at ranking, sales, and conversions. As the leading (SEO) organization at TU Enterprise, we never spend the time and money by exercising insufficient branding practices; in spite, we mainly concentrate on yielding leads and revenues for your business. Our moral (SEO) practices open new channels of sales and commerce for the job, so that you can take enough time to concentrate on your business goals. To accomplish what you need from the job, ask our (SEO) experts today.

Getting business owners involved in buying website design and (SEO) services will be challenging. Fortunately, we've produced a philosophy that not only delivers level leads but also improves exchange rates and sales. Check out our picture and see why so many network designs firms have taken our lead production companies.

(SEO) is the process that optimizes sites for web search engine ranking, making it easier for a given target audience to see the place organically. In the digital landscape, most people realize they want (SEO) for their job — but hiring somebody to do it is complex, frustrating, and may have the feeling of purchasing snake oil. After years of delivering successful (SEO) services to public and global customers, TU Enterprise and the (SEO) team decided that was the problem they would work up. What if there was one way to change people, teams, and authorities to DIY their (SEO) in a sense that's spontaneous and user-friendly?

Once again (SEO) is the marketing field focused on developing visibility in organic (non-paid) web search engine results. (SEO) encompasses both the technological and creative components needed to better rankings, drive communication, and increase awareness at search engines. There are some facets to (SEO), from those words on the page to the way other websites connect to you on the network. Sometimes (SEO) is just a matter of making sure the website is structured in a sense that search engines see. Searching for the greatest (SEO) corporations in United States? Here is the list of greatest (SEO) offices in the U.S. with customers' reviews and ratings. These tricks and tactics of (SEO) can move you ahead of this competition. When two business sites deliver the same goods or services, the company whose site in web search engine optimized will surely help in terms of greater network communication. The more of these visitors, the more possible there are chances of converting those visitors into clients resulting in sales. Thus, employing an in-house team of (SEO) experts or U.S. best (SEO) services company will become handy, (Young Entrepreneur Council., 2018).

What Tools And Software Are Used For SEO?

From 2017–2019, TU Enterprise owned just one single product — our suite of (SEO) tools and codes. Single-product corporations make marketing simple; they make building the funnel easy, they create site designing and (SEO) and knowledge strategies and team structures and news and businesses and one million other pieces of the business easier. For years, TU Enterprise benefited from these remarkable points, but we don't think we understood rather how important and friction-free it created so many aspects of the organization's development.

There are hundreds of available (SEO) tools out there, but we need to focus on just the most important to increase the toolbox. Tons of people in the (SEO) group helped vet the (SEO) code into place. To be included, it had to fulfill three requirements. How can you identify if the drop-in traffic, or change is associated with the Google Algorithm update, or maybe a better day? This is the highly recommended

Google Chrome plugin that overlays more information on top of the analytics, so you can easily send screenshots to customers showing just how right forces affects the communication.

Ahrens stands out amongst these most formal (SEO) instruments; and after Google, it is the 2nd biggest site crawler free. Since that is the greatest (SEO) investigation tool, (SEO) experts will not make enough of Ahrens Site audit tools and characteristics. These features help you determine the page of the site which requires rework to increase the ranking. It is undoubtedly the most common (SEO) tool available in this industry because of its specific and most important characteristics, like—keyword research, status tracking, competition investigation, (SEO) accounting, viral content research among others. Likewise, it lets you search where the competitors used backlinks.

SEMrush is one of the greatest (SEO) codes that every seller must-have. It conducts a complete (SEO) examination and displays the proportion of search traffic and the number of backlinks that the website has. You may still perform keyword research, subject research, and detailed competitive analysis using the tool. Log in to SEMrush and follow the realm that you want to study. This way will rapidly examine the amount of communication that the website receives, the best keywords that are sending that communication, the overall number of backlinks along with the referring domains, and the main organic competitors.

Thinking about giving backlinks to your website? Don't. Google is wiser than this, and they will take this up with you. If any (SEO) advisor tells you to use the software like that, get rid of it. If you find that black hat (SEO) is achieving individual concepts in this manner, look and see. They will be removed off Google at some point. For instance, somebody making a mobile search for the name of a restaurant is most likely after the hours, position, or list. If Someone making a background search on machines learning (SEO), is likely searching for resources and writing.

These are the main available (SEO) tools we use daily to help make our (SEO) organization campaigns more effective and effective here on Google. If you have any available (SEO) tools, like the favorite keyword instrument, keyword finder or keyword engine you need to get, please feel free to make them at *amazon.com/author/bgilmore*. Because we're constantly on this prowl for new search marketing tools and would like to learn about the favorites. Here is a good point, Keys4Up is the semantic keywords research instrument based on LSI algorithms. Keys4Up (SEO) tool helps (SEO)s, knowledge marketers and copywriters to see similar policies for any subject or niche industry. In the present's semantic (SEO) world, the usage of relevant similar statements is very crucial to make higher rankings on search engines, e.g., Google or Bing.

Competence tools/software structures – identify all these tools and software that you must achieve these techniques. (SEO) tools, PPC platforms, and third-party software, e-mail marketing platforms, video or design tools, etc.). Make sure you see this work description to see if they're searching for a person who has content with any structures or tools, such as AdWords or Photoshop.

Moz leader at (SEO) code utilizes two free (SEO) tools, Flowerhorn and Open website Explorer, have pushed tens of thousands of trails for them. Flowerhorn provides users to study their Twitter followers and make tips on developing their people. Open Site Explorer allows users to find where websites are links, which is important competitive information for any (SEO) effort. Flowerhorn also offers the ability to search for keywords in your target. Moz has always provided special tools for (SEO) and is available people. One of their newest, the Keyword Explorer, is no exception. Though few of the measures you'll take the way are related to those you'll see at Google's Keyword Planner, these are purported to be more accurate, As Google rounds its information and is not equally complete when it comes to valuing the competitor. Likewise, Moz's way can give you more detailed keyword recommendations and can qualitatively measure the cumulative amount of each keyword you follow, (DeMers, 2016).

Tiny (SEO) Tools is popular among old-time (SEO). It contains the collection of over 100 new (SEO) tools. Each instrument performs a very particular job. What's important about the publication is that additional to conventional toolsets like backlink and keyword research, you'll see the abundance of hard-to-find and specialized instruments, e.g., proxy tools, pdf tools, and even JSON tools.

Besides offering the writing detection tool, it also provides a host of additional important (SEO) tools such as section Rewriter, Keyword point, Online Ping Website means,

Backlink Checker, Backlink Maker, Link Tracker, Google PageRank Checker, Domain Authority Checker, Word Count Checker, language Checker means, and more. Grammarly gets great reviews from instructors, students, authors and professionals alike. Over 600 reputed universities believe Grammarly and millions of users use it regularly to change their work, make the new message and excel in studies and jobs.

No keywords mean that databases could take a comprehensive Keyword Planner from Google, which is a must-have for three reasons: It is from this document (Google), it's free, and it's specifically designed to give you accurate keyword information. The only catch is that it's planned for paid ad efforts (as opposed to (SEO) or content marketing efforts). Follow the handful of phrases related to the brand, and you'll be able to specify not just the search amount for those keywords, but also the comparative amount of competition that's currently fighting over them. (DeMers, J., Nov. 2016)

Take the way to the coolest toolbox. "remember somebody trying to create a building with the old education toolbox versus the tools professional contractors get on the business. A good (SEO) team comes with a significant array of code tools," and Kerns notes. These are the important tools of this (SEO) business. Yet if you knew exactly what to obtain, they'd cost you tens of thousands of dollars to buy, often less usage." (Harrison, K., May. 2017)

Some of the marketing code we've developed in recent years has a specific purpose. Imagine social and optimization or (SEO) backlink analytics. Even if some of these tools have a narrow use, it does not think that there are dependencies between organizations or chances to change workflows. (Waite, M., Jan. 2017)

What makes SEO And PPC different?

As a CEO of the network design business that runs with best customers across Canada, we needed to spread this word about how (SEO) lends the side with brand awareness, website traffic, PPC and lead generation, (Sharma, 2018).

Hemolysis is best for PPC education at Indore along with documentation and (SEO) education. Our trainers are Google certified and have wide content running on the current PPC method for years. Our PPC education association at Indore has had paid account form Google to do learned forms on this. We do make 100 percent placement help naturally to all participants. PPC (earnings per click) is a paid marketing tool invented to increase communication to the site. It is the most common and demanding marketing device used by authorities to make online profiles without looking for periods. They will take

PPC for least 15 times in a month and must pay ahead of time.

The crucial situation here is to see the change between (SEO) and PPC. (SEO) is made to improve the organic/natural search rankings, and PPC represents the given efforts that you work online to attract visitors. You need to make a good balance between (SEO) and PPC marketing techniques to take related traffic to the site. Additionally, there are some places where PPC (the element of (SEM) makes more meaning than (SEO). For instance, if you are first establishing the website and you need quick clarity, it is a great idea to make a PPC campaign because it takes less time than (SEO), but it would be foolish to strictly get with PPC and not even have web search engine optimization.

PPC will be treated very differently from the (SEO) plan. First, PPC is the short-term program — you will take the

PPC plan on and away as you wish and swiftly optimize accounts for success. PPC aims to get customers to the site almost instantly and can be controlled according to trends in the business. You will become intelligent with the PPC plan. Here are a few situations you can secure; you can give the price of the keywords and be aggressive at your fields. Recognize seasonal trends and allow your budget to fluctuate to match this demand. You can align the PPC budget to your business goals throughout the year

Often, web search engine optimization (SEO) is considered something that you can find in a different environment than pay-per-click (PPC). Nevertheless, some people are unaware of the possibilities these two have when placed together. There is no doubt that (SEO) and PPC will create a good team. This is supported by the absolute potential of having more.

We think PPC is just being used by corporations to keep others from ranking, given they have never used legit

(SEO). We believe it's more of the competitor than someone providing a good PPC advertising, it’s only to make communication on their site to make their ranking more related.

Using the priority list, gives these meta titles more (SEO) friendly results. This may include applying target keywords earlier or making the name more attractive. See from successful PPC advertising lessons: Marketing teams spend a lot of time in optimizing PPC advertisements for CTR and would probably have higher CTR. Meta descriptions represent one of the most important elements at CTR. Make sure to add the clear call to action, as the correct keyword expression you need to rank for. Do not leave to set searcher intent: For instance, the term “greatest tools for increasing organic communication” has the informational and list meaning behind it.

For some corporations, pay per click ad is a complement to their (SEO) campaigns that gain outcomes in the long-term, while PPC will bring outcomes in the short-term since they are paid for. (SEO) may be easily described as the oven since it heats up for a period and becomes awhile before it is turn down. PPC is more like the microwave that heats up rapidly and chills down rapidly. When spending on PPC the ads go on now, but they take off even as quickly when the effort is full, losing all the organization's rankings for specific keywords that were paid for through PPC.

PPC creates instantaneous amounts of alas, these figures may be misleading and don't necessarily change to sales. Yet when they do, when looking at these figures, PPC stays logical, but never increases in quantity, while SEO strategy and social media finally exceed PPC at quantity exponentially over time, something depicted in the graphic below.

The best method seems to be for the PPC campaign to speed up the launch of the (SEO) strategy and social media strategy. It is crucial not to trust the PPC effort and learn to change. At the time you stop spending money on PPC, the online presence evaporates. The best solution to any disagreement is to find the way to get into (SEO). Therefore, advertising uses the radical marketing strategy that harnesses the power of both companies. Number Advertising still provides a commission-based pay system that means you just spend on the service when you get the sale.

It is cost-effective – Compared to the prices associated with different kinds of online commerce, e.g., PPC advertising, social media selling, or purchase leads for the e-mail marketing system, (SEO) provides good ROI. While PPC may run more income and social media may be more valuable for the example, the organic (SEO) in some ways remains the bedrock of your online existence.

Offer the same services to (SEO) Shark regarding web search engine optimization, PPC and social media, although with less emphasis on-site design and on-page optimization. The disagreement with this concern, however, is that they provide education to their customers, so that they are equipped to get their (SEO) campaigns up and running.

The greatest (SEO) efforts can add site optimization, link business, message work, keywords, PPC and social media is what you make with (SEO) Shark. It may take a couple of months to begin realizing the perfect results, but once you do so the page visitors, inquiries and income will all change. Foxtail commerce – https://foxtailmarketing.com, established in 2010, is a massive digital marketing business that provides companies ranging from (SEO) to technical content marketing. They tend to specialize in B2B (commerce to commerce) and SaaS (package as the service) selling, and they have produced very powerful techniques for these types of (SEO).

Web nemesis constitutes this greatest SEO education at TU Enterprise with positioning and certification. This (SEO)

PPC education is for all freshmen at Beech College and working professionals who need to develop business in the digital marketing world. We have been ranked at the top 10 (SEO) education associations at TU Enterprise because of our level, education, dedication, and consistent results. Within (SEO) courses we take on PPC, Google AdWords, on author (SEO), Off author (SEO), and infographics. Our program is planned by experts giving 5 years of experience in (SEO) education. We begin with basics and gradually go forward with more advanced techniques.

AQABA technology is the Google AdWords Certified Partner and the (SEO), Digital Marketing and Web Design company, established at Sterling Heights, Chicago. They are one of the leading ad agencies in this country, providing complete (SEO) & PPC services, digital marketing, and network innovation — along with a host of different services. We would like to speak to you about (SEO) services, and digital marketing needs and goals.

Iron paper is the digital marketing business established in NYC. We specialize in multi-channel, integrated commerce, including (SEO), PPC, promotion, cultural and content. Our capabilities with web design, engineering, commerce, and integrated digital strategy make us a trusted person for commerce and organization efforts. Our method allows us to combine both digital efforts with traditional marketing to produce a good marketing mix.

Some digital marketing specialists choose to concentrate on one field, e.g., (SEO), paid search (PPC), display media, content marketing, or social media. Digital marketing specialists have a different and ever-evolving skill set and to be productive are required to change with these times as marketing and engineering effects. As with most commerce roles, digital commerce specialists make standard business hours. Because of the online nature of their business, working remotely is also a powerful prospect. The primary character is to make and implement digital marketing efforts to support company marketing and advertising targets.

SPINX Digital is the digital marketing business that provides creative web design and development, social media selling, PPC, (SEO), e-mail marketing and television production companies. Unlike other offices, SPINX specializes in individual experience and visual design to make the site visually fascinating, engaging for visitors, and optimized for transformation. Prefer SPINX Digital if you have a visible brand and want assistance with the design and functionality of the site.

Great Like medium offers business, tailored solutions in web design, software development, and digital commerce. With the devoted and knowledgeable team of (SEO), PPC, cultural media, graphic designing, and planning professionals, our expertise stems from this concept that we would see day’s technologies while also having over a decade of experience in our respective niche.

Sleight ad is a digital marketing business that has the education, expertise, and award-winning affects you want to make 2020 the breakout year. With broad content in SEO, PPC, social media and network innovation, their experts can be with you every step of this way. It all begins with the strong formula that our digital marketing strategists have developed for tremendous business development.

Network Marketing is additionally divided into several administrations which include, (SEO) (web search engine streamlining), SMO (Social Media Optimization), PPC (earnings Per stop), Affiliate Marketing, Email Marketing, and few others. Among these governments, (SEO) is significantly used by all the enterprises which rely on network guests. We are offering Digital commerce services at TU Enterprise.

Some time ago, three people who had been allies to ages, joined and made the corporation. Algorithm Digital selling result was born. Located in Sydney, Australia they offer (SEO) services, e.g., (SEO), PPC, digital marketing schemes and social media schemes for sites. Their organization has enjoyed considerable success, and this corporation has consistently been ranked as one of the best (SEO) corporations in the country. Amir Nothani is the expert manager of Algorithm Digital selling Solutions, while Sam Prince is the Managing manager, and Leila Dorati is the chief of accounting organization.

Digital Vidya – You will also join the Digital Vidya to see strategies for Digital commerce. It can tell you on the network and online offline digital marketing classes. At Digital Vidya, you will see about (SEO), SMO, PPC, and Digital Marketing systems through various education meetings. DTI – digital Technology association (DTI) is also a not too bad organization for extensive learning of digital commerce. The experienced force of DTI is always ready to inspire you. At DTI, you can take central knowledge of Digital commerce. It is equally situated in Janakpur and Saket.

Digital commerce INDORE provides its clients complete results for digital commerce, including the design and developing of sites, e-commerce solutions, (SEO), SMO, PPC, online reputation management, content design and marketing, graphic design. Our established business results allow us to produce a coherent and clean experience for our potential customers.

Managing the digital ad in-house may make it extreme to use all these digital communications available to improve the business. You may need assistance with SMO, PPC campaigns, (SEO), e-mail records, social networking campaigns, but with one in-house person, it is challenging to become smooth and result driven. Outsourcing will give you the chance to use other advertising channels effortlessly. You may use the creator to refresh the website, the publicist to sell with the blog or e-mail pamphlet, and a web-based social networking professional to secure SMO. In comparison, while you want to employ employees to perform (SEO) and possibly invest in (SEO) products, (SEO) itself is available and will help you organically get to your goal audience over the long-term. PPC and e-mail marketing have cheap set-ups and would be anywhere from a couple of cents per stop to a couple of bucks. Conventional television advertisement lets you transmit to anyone who turns on this line. To get an audience to whom the product can challenge, you need to think about what kind of television programming might appeal to the perfect demographic -- it's difficult to apply or collect any audience-specific analytics.

How Much Can You Expect to Pay for SEO Services?

Seeing deeper: The (SEO) value may imply one of two things: The investing in the organic search strategy, or how much you spend on paid web search engine commerce; (SEM) services like Google AdWords. If you're paying for a tool, consultant, or marketing agency to help you modify the network content, the statement will differ widely with the level of the companies you're receiving.

How web search engine optimization will help you present, valuable tips. (SEO) Services can be defined as a series of methods to help improve the profile the site in web search engine lists. While coding this feign; inelab.gachon.Ac.kr, idea, the creator should pay attention to the heading tag. If you are today going by the Internet marketing effort or are relating to get alongside on the Internet marketing effort, one idea you cannot afford to give back on is search engine optimization (SEO).

The reason you want it: (SEO) is no longer optional. It is required, especially if you're running the trade site. (SEO) is a series of tasks that finally determines where the site places on search engines for a specific keyword. The idea is that the site should be that people look high above others if the search for a specialty is questioned. How much you'll give: (SEO) prices differ per business, but it is one of the pricier expenses of things related to running the site. The bigger the organization, the higher you will consider costs to be. How much you'll give: (SEO) is an on-going action, it's never a one-time thing.

If you must take an extra $ 25,000 per month in extra income, you cannot just give $ 500 for it. This is the thought as to how the industry works. Different Las Vegas (SEO)s can pay you smaller sums to do (SEO) jobs, but what they are not telling you is that you would not remain capable to outrank those top-ranking businesses that are paying thousands for (SEO) services. There is no way you will succeed on getting their rankings without investing a similar amount that were put into the better grade of Las Vegas (SEO).

Out of all the Las Vegas (SEO) corporations, we try hard to explain how (SEO) works. Other Las Vegas (SEO) companies are expecting to get the fast buck by luring you into giving them a monthly charge for usually at least a one-year bid. Once you contract, they normally can outsource the business to a much cheaper company so they will turn into the middleman. We have yet gotten these Las Vegas (SEO) corporations to contact us to take their grunt men and make them seem better.

Dozens of people applying for our assistance quit their part time jobs to start-up (SEO) jobs that relied almost solely on our delivery. Our biggest consumer, the (SEO) organization that provided honor management services for celebrities in the UK, was giving us $ 1,000 one month and likely pointing its customers up to 50 to 100 times more than that.

We just realized how heavily they were balling when they showed up on this Inc. 500 database in 2017.

As Google extends to unhinge selling models everywhere, corporations are increasing expenditure on digital marketing companies. If you are considering investing in web search engine optimization (SEO), it may be difficult to determine where to spend money, particularly when selling budgets are usually hard. However, (SEO) firms may have a lot of value in the business, and some marketers are taking the plunge. According to media analysts in Borrell, (SEO) expenditure can become an $ 80 billion industry yearly by 2020, (Harrison, 2017). You most likely landed on my author page by exploring the period (aka key term or keyword) at Google, something like: " *amazon.com/author/bgilmore* ", "(SEO) company books ", " (SEO) search engine optimization ", " localized (SEO) *amazon.com/author/bgilmore* books on (SEO) ", " greatest (SEO) corporations" (all of which we grade for) , or And the second reason: We obviously, know what we are doing. We learn how to grade for key terms. We mean, but consider it, we are ranked at the best results for Amazon books on (SEO) amazon.com/author/bgilmore with various (SEO) book corporations. This is not a simple task to do, one, because we represent so-called experts, and two, it's darn aggressive.

Thank you for reading our Search Engine Optimization (SEO) book, this book is so important for the (SEO) effort because with this book all backlink knowledge from beginning to finish would take autopilot. Veazie Gilmore spent around 12 months producing this fully automated (SEO) book you can find this book at the button below for more information, also take this book with a discount at tuenterprise.com or *amazon.com/author/bgilmore*.

ONLINE
MARKETING
S.E.O
Content
Lists
Links
Titles
Blogs
Sales

Resources

"Intro to Search Engine Optimization | Search Engine Watch". *searchenginewatch.com*. Retrieved 2017-06-29.

Danny Sullivan (June 14, 2004). "Who Invented the Term "Search Engine Optimization"?". Search Engine Watch. Archived from the original on 23 April 2010. Retrieved May 14, 2007. See Google groups thread.

"Trade Name Certification". State of Arizona.

Cho, J., Garcia-Molina, H. (1998). "Efficient crawling through URL ordering". Proceedings of the seventh conference on World Wide Web, Brisbane, Australia. Retrieved May 9, 2007. CS1 maint: Multiple names: authors list (link)

"Google's Guidelines on Site Design". google.com. Retrieved April 18, 2007.

"Bing Webmaster Guidelines". bing.com. Retrieved September 11, 2014.

Matt Cutts (February 4, 2006). "Ramping up on international web spam". mattcutts.com/blog. Retrieved May 9, 2007.

Matt Cutts (February 7, 2006). "Recent reclusions". mattcutts.com/blog. Retrieved May 9, 2007.

"Technology & Marketing Law Blog: Kinder Start v. Google Dismissed—With Sanctions Against Kinder Start's Counsel". blog.ericgoldman.org. Retrieved June 23, 2008.

"Search King, Inc. v. Google Technology, Inc., CIV-02-1457-M" (PDF). docstoc.com. May 27, 2003. Retrieved May 23, 2008.

Stefanie Olsen (May 30, 2003). "Judge dismisses suit against Google". CNET. Retrieved May 10, 2007.

David Kesmodel (September 22, 2005). "Sites Get Dropped by Search Engines After Trying to 'Optimize' Rankings". *Wall Street Journal*. Retrieved July 30, 2008.

Adam L. Penenberg (September 8, 2005). "Legal Showdown in Search Fracas". Wired Magazine. Retrieved August 11, 2016.

Matt Cutts (February 2, 2006). "Confirming a penalty". mattcutts.com/blog. Retrieved May 9, 2007.

"Microsoft hits search deal with Opera Software".

"Bing Introducing Firefox with Bing". Bing. Archived from the original on December 4, 2011. Retrieved December 16, 2011.

Mozilla. "Offering a Customized Firefox Experience for Bing Users". Mozilla. Retrieved December 16, 2011.

jsullivan. "Refreshing the Firefox Search Bar". Mozilla. Retrieved December 16, 2011.

"Mobile-first Index". Google.com. Retrieved March 19, 2018.

"SEO". Definition.net. Retrieved March 19, 2018.

Gray, M. (Jun. 2018). Why Search Engine Optimization Is Not A One-Time Event. *Forbes*. Retrieved from https://www.forbes.com/sites/forbesagencycouncil/2018/06/25/why-search-engine-optimization-is-not-a-one-time-event/

Brown, M. S. (Mar. 2018). Get the Basics on NoSQL Databases: Search Engine Databases. *Forbes*. Retrieved from https://www.forbes.com/sites/metabrown/2018/03/31/get-the-basics-on-nosql-databases-search-engine-databases/

Gray, M. (Jun. 2018). Why Search Engine Optimization Is Not A One-Time Event. *Forbes*. Retrieved from https://www.forbes.com/sites/forbesagencycouncil/2018/06/25/why-search-engine-optimization-is-not-a-one-time-event/

"FAQ". Rank Star. Retrieved 19 June 2013.

See, Dianne (January 7, 2009). "Microsoft Beats Out Google To Win Verizon Search Deal". Moco News. Retrieved December 16, 2011.

"As Verizon Implements Bing Default Search Deal, Company Sees User Backlash". Searchengineland.com. Retrieved December 16, 2011.

Olenski, S. (Jun. 2018). 5 Search Engine Optimization Tips All CMOs Need to Understand. *Forbes*. Retrieved from https://www.forbes.com/sites/steveolenski/2018/06/27/5-search-engine-optimization-tips-all-cmos-need-to-understand/

"Bing Unleashing Tiger to Speed Search Results". Search Engine Watch. 30 September 2011. Retrieved 3 October 2011.

Goldman, David (May 10, 2012). "Bing fires at Google with new social search". CNN Money. Retrieved May 10, 2012.

Yang, X. S., & Deb, S. (2010). Engineering optimization by cuckoo search. *International Journal of Mathematical Modelling and Numerical Optimization*, *1*(4), 330–343.

Brin, Sergey & Page, Larry (1998). "The Anatomy of a Large-Scale Hypertextual Web Search Engine". Proceedings of the seventh international conference on World Wide Web. pp. 107–117. Retrieved May 8, 2007.

"RFC 812 - NICNAME/WHOIS". *ietf.org*.

"Knowbot programming: System support for mobile agents". *cnri.reston.va.us*.

Deutsch, Peter (September 11, 1990). "[next] An Internet archive server (was about Lisp)". *groups.google.com*. Retrieved 2017-12-29.

Sharma, K. (Jul. 2018). How SEO And Content Marketing Work Together to Fuel Your Online Success. *Forbes*. Retrieved from

https://www.forbes.com/sites/forbesagencycouncil/2018/07/03/how-seo-and-content-marketing-work-together-to-fuel-your-online-success/

Yang, X. S., & Deb, S. (2010). Engineering optimization by cuckoo search. *International Journal of Mathematical Modelling and Numerical Optimization*, *1*(4), 330–343.

Brin, Sergey & Page, Larry (1998). "The Anatomy of a Large-Scale Hypertextual Web Search Engine". Proceedings of the seventh international conference on World Wide Web. pp. 107–117. Retrieved May 8, 2007.

"RFC 812 - NICNAME/WHOIS". *ietf.org*.

"Knowbot programming: System support for mobile agents". *cnri.reston.va.us*.

Deutsch, Peter (September 11, 1990). "[next] An Internet archive server (was about Lisp)". *groups.google.com*. Retrieved 2017-12-29.

Sharma, K. (Jul. 2018). How SEO And Content Marketing Work Together to Fuel Your Online Success. *Forbes*. Retrieved from https://www.forbes.com/sites/forbesagencycouncil/2018/07/03/how-seo-and-content-marketing-work-together-to-fuel-your-online-success/

"False Oracles: Consumer Reaction to Learning the Truth About How Search Engines Work (Abstract)". consumerwebwatch.org. June 30, 2003. Retrieved 2007-06-09.

"Searching for Disclosure: How Search Engines Alert Consumers to the Presence of Advertising in Search Results". consumerwebwatch.org. November 8, 2004. Retrieved 2007-06-09.

"Still in Search of Disclosure: Re-evaluating How Search Engines Explain the Presence of Advertising in Search Results". consumerwebwatch.org. June 9, 2005. Retrieved 2007-06-09.

"Re: Complaint Requesting Investigation of Various Internet Search Engine Companies for Paid Placement or (Pay per click)". ftc.gov. June 22, 2002. Archived from the original on July 23, 2013. Retrieved 2007-06-09.

Anderson, T. (Jan. 2014). Choose your weapon: SEO or social media? *The Guardian*. Retrieved from https://www.theguardian.com/technology/2014/jan/06/seo-or-social-media

Rampton, J. (Sep. 2016). 20 Reasons Your Business Is Failing At SEO, And How to Fix. *Forbes*. Retrieved from https://www.forbes.com/sites/johnrampton/2016/09/14/20-reasons-your-business-is-failing-at-seo-and-how-to-fix/

DeMers, J. (Jan. 2014). The Three Pillars of SEO in 2014. *Forbes*. Retrieved from http://www.forbes.com/sites/jaysondemers/2014/01/28/the-three-pillars-of-seo-in-2014/

Pinsky, D. (Jun. 2017). Google Says: Here's What to Look for In an SEO Firm. *Forbes*. Retrieved from https://www.forbes.com/sites/denispinsky/2017/06/19/how-to-hire-seo/

The Economist. (Jun. 2017). China's new cyber-security law is worryingly vague. *The Economist*. Retrieved from https://www.economist.com/news/business/21722873-its-rules-are-broad-ambiguous-and-bothersome-international-firms-chinas-new-cyber-security

Control Risks. (May. 2017). China's Cyber Security Law: The Impossibility of Compliance? *Forbes*. Retrieved from https://www.forbes.com/sites/riskmap/2017/05/29/chinas-cyber-security-law-the-impossibility-of-compliance/

"Mikko Hypponen: Fighting viruses, defending the net". TED. Archived from the original on 16 January 2013.

"Mikko Hypponen – Behind Enemy Lines". Hack in The Box Security Conference. Archived from the original on 25 November 2016.

Skroupa, C. P. (Feb. 2018). An Approach 'Essential to Creating Robust, Sustainable Cyber Security' *Forbes*. Retrieved from https://www.forbes.com/sites/christopherskroupa/2018/02/27/an-approach-essential-to-creating-robust-sustainable-cyber-security/

Wintermeyer, L. (May. 2017). Cyber - The Threat Is Real. *Forbes*. Retrieved from https://www.forbes.com/sites/lawrencewintermeyer/2017/05/03/cyber-the-threat-is-real/

Reuters. (Jun. 2016). Congress Investigating Federal Reserve Cyber Breaches Over 'Serious Concerns' *Fortune*. Retrieved from http://fortune.com/2016/06/03/federal-reserve-cyber-breaches/

Beshar, P. J. (Nov. 2016). Why New Regulations Won't Scare Off Cyber Hacks. *Fortune*. Retrieved from http://fortune.com/2016/11/29/donald-trump-cybersecurity/

Patel, N. (Apr. 2016). The Entrepreneur's SEO Survival Guide For 2016. *Forbes*. Retrieved from https://www.forbes.com/sites/neilpatel/2016/04/01/the-entrepreneurs-seo-survival-guide-for-2016/

DeMers, J. (Mar. 2018). Is There Any New Innovation In SEO? *Forbes*. Retrieved from https://www.forbes.com/sites/jaysondemers/2018/03/02/is-there-any-new-innovation-in-seo/

Shorr, B. (Jul. 2018). 6 Reasons Why SEO Might Not Be Right for Your Business. *Forbes*. Retrieved from https://www.forbes.com/sites/allbusiness/2018/07/12/reasons-seo-not-right-for-your-business/

Adams. (May. 2016). Three SEO Strategies to Get Your Startup Off the Ground. *Forbes*. Retrieved from https://www.forbes.com/sites/robertadams/2016/05/31/three-seo-strategies-to-get-your-startup-off-the-ground/

Patel, N. (Apr. 2016). The Entrepreneur's SEO Survival Guide For 2016. *Forbes*. Retrieved from https://www.forbes.com/sites/neilpatel/2016/04/01/the-entrepreneurs-seo-survival-guide-for-2016/

Harrison, K. (May. 2017). Why Investing in SEO Makes Good Business Sense? *Forbes*. Retrieved from https://www.forbes.com/sites/kateharrison/2017/05/19/why-investing-in-seo-makes-good-business-sense/

Patel, N. (Apr. 2016). The Entrepreneur's SEO Survival Guide For 2016. *Forbes*. Retrieved from https://www.forbes.com/sites/neilpatel/2016/04/01/the-entrepreneurs-seo-survival-guide-for-2016/

Gleeson, B. (Apr. 2015). 7 Bold Statements About The 10 Year Forecast For SEO. *Forbes*. Retrieved from https://www.forbes.com/sites/brentgleeson/2015/04/06/7-bold-statements-about-the-10-year-forecast-for-seo/

Pinsky, D. (Jun. 2017). Google Says: Here's What to Look for In an SEO Firm. *Forbes*. Retrieved from https://www.forbes.com/sites/denispinsky/2017/06/19/how-to-hire-seo/

Willi, S. (Sep. 2017). SEO Friendly Website Design: Building A Strong Foundation for Search. *Forbes*. Retrieved from https://www.forbes.com/sites/forbesagencycouncil/2017/09/26/seo-friendly-website-design-building-a-strong-foundation-for-search/

Nadeem, S (2009) Macaulay's (Cyber) Children: The Cultural Politics of Outsourcing in India Archived 2010-06-20 at the Way back Machine. Cultural Sociology.

Patel, N. (Jun. 2016). 6 Outsourcing Tips to Add Nuclear Power to Your Content Marketing. *Forbes*. Retrieved from https://www.forbes.com/sites/neilpatel/2016/06/16/6-outsourcing-tips-to-add-nuclear-power-to-your-content-marketing/

"5 Facts About Overseas Outsourcing". *Center for American Progress*. 2012-07-09. Retrieved 2018-05-31.

"Here, There and Everywhere". *The Economist [London] n.d.: n. pag. 17 January 2013. Archived from the original on 18 January 2013. Retrieved 19 January 2013.*

Blasingame, J. (Feb. 2016). Are You Asking the Outsourcing Power Question? *Forbes*. Retrieved from https://www.forbes.com/sites/jimblasingame/2016/02/26/are-you-asking-the-outsourcing-power-question/

(Jul. 2018). Search engine. *Britannica*. Retrieved from www.britannica.com/technology/search-engine

Matthews, C. (Jun. 2015). France orders Google to delete even more stuff from search results. *Fortune*. Retrieved from http://fortune.com/2015/06/12/france-google-search/

Luckerson, V. (Jun. 2015). Google Will Remove Revenge Porn from Search Results. *Time*. Retrieved from http://time.com/3928830/google-revenge-porn-remove/

Rampton, J. (Dec. 2016). Tweets in Google Search: Google Sharpens the Focus. *Forbes*. Retrieved from https://www.forbes.com/sites/johnrampton/2016/12/08/tweets-in-google-search-google-sharpens-the-focus/

Roberts, J. J. (Dec. 2016). A Top Google Result for the Holocaust Is Now a White Supremacist Site. *Fortune*. Retrieved from http://fortune.com/2016/12/12/google-holocaust/

Steimle, J. (Feb. 2015). How Long Does SEO Take to Start Working? *Forbes*. Retrieved from http://www.forbes.com/sites/joshsteimle/2015/02/07/how-long-does-seo-take-to-start-working/

Steimle, J. (Feb. 2015). How Long Does SEO Take to Start Working? *Forbes*. Retrieved from http://www.forbes.com/sites/joshsteimle/2015/02/07/how-long-does-seo-take-to-start-working/

Lashinsky, A. (Sep. 2010). Ning CEO: Building a better web site. *Fortune*. Retrieved from http://fortune.com/2010/09/27/ning-ceo-building-a-better-web-site/

Atal, M. (Aug. 2009). Meet "the world's most annoying Web site" *Fortune*. Retrieved from http://fortune.com/2009/08/07/meet-the-worlds-most-annoying-web-site/

Patel, N. (Apr. 2016). The Entrepreneur's SEO Survival Guide For 2016. *Forbes*. Retrieved from https://www.forbes.com/sites/neilpatel/2016/04/01/the-entrepreneurs-seo-survival-guide-for-2016/

Shorr, B. (Jul. 2018). 6 Reasons Why SEO Might Not Be Right for Your Business. *Forbes*. Retrieved from https://www.forbes.com/sites/allbusiness/2018/07/12/reasons-seo-not-right-for-your-business/

Young Entrepreneur Council. (Jun. 2018). Best Ways to Improve Your SEO And Why You Need to Do It. *Forbes*. Retrieved from https://www.forbes.com/sites/theyec/2018/06/11/best-ways-to-improve-your-seo-and-why-you-need-to-do-it/

Harrison, K. (May. 2017). Why Investing in SEO Makes Good Business Sense? *Forbes*. Retrieved from https://www.forbes.com/sites/kateharrison/2017/05/19/why-investing-in-seo-makes-good-business-sense/

Waite, M. (Jan. 2017). How to Get the Most Out of Your Marketing Analytics Tools. *Fortune*. Retrieved from http://fortune.com/2017/01/30/marketing-analytics-tools/

Sharma, K. (Jul. 2018). How SEO And Content Marketing Work Together to Fuel Your Online Success. *Forbes*. Retrieved from https://www.forbes.com/sites/forbesagencycouncil/2018/07/03/how-seo-and-content-marketing-work-together-to-fuel-your-online-success/

Harrison, K. (May. 2017). Why Investing in SEO Makes Good Business Sense? *Forbes*. Retrieved from https://www.forbes.com/sites/kateharrison/2017/05/19/why-investing-in-seo-makes-good-business-sense/

www.ingramcontent.com/pod-product-compliance
Lightning Source LLC
Chambersburg PA
CBHW061344250726
48657CB00004B/1328